YOU'RE NOT
ROB SNARSKI

About the Author

Rob Snarski is a singer, a velvet-voiced troubadour.

His musical life began as a ten-year-old, playing a very heavy 120 button accordion gifted to him by his grandmother. He took up the guitar in his teens and formed Chad's Tree in the 1980's with his singer, songwriter brother Mark.

Chad's Tree released two albums, *Buckle in the Rail* and *Kerosene* along with several singles before Rob left to pursue his interest in words and melodies. He found his voice and the spotlight with part-time, holiday-band The Bottomless Schooners of Old, featuring members of The Triffids, later going on to share vocal duties with David McComb in The Blackeyed Susans and singing the songs penned by McComb and founding member Phil Kakulas. Later, he took on the craft of song-writing himself. He has written and co-written songs on The Blackeyed Susans releases *Mouth to Mouth*, *Spin The Bottle*, *La Mascara*, *Shangri-La* and *Close Your Eyes and See* and has released several solo CDs and duo recordings – *There Is Nothing Here That Belongs To You* with Dan Luscombe, his acclaimed solo debut *Wounded Bird* and the album of cover versions, *Low Fidelity* (Songs By Request), recorded at home in the hills of Tecoma on a trusty iphone.

Rob has toured the globe with The Blackeyed Susans and as a guest vocalist with The Triffids and has graced the same stage as Johnny Cash, Leonard Cohen and Nico amongst others not quite as popular.

YOU'RE NOT ROB SNARSKI
Crumbs from the cake

ROB SNARSKI

First published in 2017 by
UWA Publishing
Crawley, Western Australia 6009
www.uwap.uwa.edu.au

UWAP is an imprint of UWA Publishing,
a division of The University of Western Australia.

This book is copyright. Apart from any fair dealing for the purpose of private study, research, criticism or review, as permitted under the Copyright Act 1968, no part may be reproduced by any process without written permission. Enquiries should be made to the publisher.

Copyright © Rob Snarski 2017

The moral right of the author has been asserted.

National Library of Australia Cataloguing-in-Publication entry

Creator: Snarski, Rob, author.
You're not Rob Snarski : crumbs from the cake / Rob Snarski.
ISBN: 9781742589282 (paperback)
Snarski, Rob.
Singers—Australia—Biography.
Entertainers—Biography.
Lyricists—Australia—Biography.
Musicians—Biography.

Typeset by Lasertype
Printed by Lightning Source
Cover design by Alissa Dinallo

Contents

Author's Note	vii
You're Not Rob Snarski	1
Wounded Bird	3
The Orchard	6
Johnny Cash	9
Birth	13
Chad's Tree	15
Roleystone Pool	18
The Triffids	21
Lambsie	24
The Go-Betweens	27
The Accordion	30
Under 14s Football	34
Susie the Bush Kangaroo	37
The Fonz	39
The Reels	41
Laughing Clowns	44
David and Margaret	48
The Aurora Nightclub	52
The Birthday Party and Jonathan Richman	54
Morrissey Road Party	57
The Moodists	61
Phil Kakulas	63

CONTENTS

The Marrickville Postman	66
The Velvet Underground and Nico	69
Paul Kelly	72
Casino Lights	76
Ocean of You	79
Pig and Salmon	82
Sing the Song	85
First Song	88
Jim and Warren	92
The Punter's Club	97
Babcia	100
An Incident in Glebe	103
Pizza Guy	106
Father	109
Honey	112
Leonard Cohen	115
Moomoo	118
Pigeons and Absinthe	120
Eyjafjallajökull	124
Christmas	127
Hometown Farewells	132
Live	135
Alcohol	137
Golden Boy	139
Pledge	141
Writing songs	145
Caravan Music Club	147
Acknowledgements	151
Photographic acknowledgements	152

Author's Note

I never intended to write a book. Never intended to compile short snippets of recollections and find appropriate photographs to sit beside them within a paper framework. A book was never part of the plan. I'd barely scraped through English in the final years of high school; comprehension was never a favourite of mine.

All this came about through a friend who read some of my reminiscing one morning on social media and insisted I send it on to a publisher he knew.

The majority of these recollections were written on a train or a plane, in a hotel room or airport lounge. There's something about being in motion, in-between places that helps jolt my memory. Random thoughts spill out when I'm travelling from home in the hills of Tecoma to my part-time day jobs in town or when flying out from Melbourne to other destinations for music.

There are some chapters within that are possibly too private. I grappled with the notion of including them, precariously I let go, I'm still not quite sure why.

The collection is sporadic, arbitrary with a gap or two. They are my memories of events and I imagine may differ slightly to others present at the time. I couldn't simply write about all things music and only music, as other experiences and beings shape my existence.

You're Not Rob Snarski

'You're not Rob Snarski,' said the young boy staring up at me. He sounded certain, looked slightly puzzled and more than a little disappointed by my existence.

'Yes, I am. It's just I've gone and grown a moustache and I'm wearing glasses,' I responded, not exactly sounding sure of myself.

'No. You're not Rob Snarski,' he repeated, convinced I wasn't me, staring deep past my spectacles.

It was an awkward, perplexing moment and this little kid was making me feel just a tad anxious. Maybe I'm not Rob Snarski …but then again, why am I standing here in the middle of Readings Bookstore, Carlton, with a guitar slung over my shoulder, singing songs from *Wounded Bird* and *Low Fidelity*, alongside the travel section, on a makeshift stage whilst everyone else is sampling the free wine and flicking through the CD racks grazing for a new purchase.

After I sang six songs or so, trying to convince myself I was who I thought I was, the boy again came up to me.

'Okay, you are Rob Snarski. Thanks for singing "The Black Caress", that's my favourite.'

Then he followed with some quick-fire questions: 'What's your favourite song? Who's your favourite band? Are you your favourite singer?'

Woah, let me have a think about all that.

He told me he liked Queen and 'Bohemian Rhapsody' was his favourite song of all time (hmm, quite an epic for a lad of ten, I thought). His mother and I then began chatting, discussing the possibility of an acoustic house concert, and before I had the chance to notice, everyone else in the shop who'd come to hear some songs had drifted off into the night and I remained standing there, wondering if I was who I think I am.

Low Fidelity collage by Fiona McMonagle.

Wounded Bird

Wounded Bird had a very difficult birth. I'd never experienced as many things going belly up with a recording to this point in time. It was exhausting, a little sad and at times unbearable. Corrupt hard drives, stolen computers, stalled sessions: hours of lost recordings, gone forever.

Having said all that, it blossomed over time and became a stronger record due to the distress it caused and its tumultuous nature. I'd run out of funds, the publisher lost interest and I was left with a sketch: a sloppy, join-the-dots train-wreck sketch. I'd been working with Dan Luscombe on this new recording intermittently; he was extremely busy, squeezing in time whenever he could. It was intended to be a follow-up to our album *There Is Nothing Here That Belongs to You*. It's always difficult and sometimes a little complicated when close musician friends have more pressing priorities. Dan was immersed in the music world. He'd been playing with Paul Kelly, Dan Kelly and The Drones, as well as producing film soundtracks, on top of working with rising uber-starlet Courtney Barnett. So in the scheme of things, the pile was large and I was lost deep amongst it all, somewhere near the bottom. If it wasn't for the crowd-funding campaign instigated by all-round nice guy Andrew Fuller, I'd still be mumbling to myself, curled up in a ball on a footpath somewhere.

Dan and I had started to work with Shane O'Mara at his Tuscan villa–style studio – Yikesville, in downtown Yarraville. It was at the back of his house, a little recording oasis with an endless array of guitars, amps and effects pedals, hidden amongst Mexicana memorabilia and a collection of empty tequila bottles. I'd seen Shane play over the years with Chris Wilson, Paul Kelly, Stephen Cummings, Rebecca's Empire and Edwyn Collins. I enjoyed his production work, especially on Lisa Miller recordings. He was relaxed, open to any creative ideas thrown his way: a positive person with realistic and sensible working hours - five or six hours a day was more than enough.

After one of the sessions with Shane and negotiating traffic back to music headquarters in Northcote, Dan quietly confessed that he thought this should be my solo record: the songs were mine; it was more me, less him. It was a sensible and a reasonable suggestion but at that precise moment it felt like a slap in the face, an insult. I avoided running into the oncoming traffic and had a think about it - I was taken aback, never having considered this idea before.

Over the coming months I simply accepted this as a gift from Dan. No longer would I have to rely on him quite as much, I could simply go about finishing this flightless bird with whoever was keen and available. Dan contributed a lot to the recording and to the arrangements of songs but paradoxically that brief conversation gave me the opportunity to reclaim and focus on the songs and what remained to be done.

Wounded Bird painting by Sandra Eterovic.

The Orchard

My working life began around about the ripe old age of eight. My parents had acquired a property in Karragullen on the cusp of the Perth metropolitan area, off the Brookton Highway, up in the Darling Ranges.

Eighty-nine acres all up, with ten acres of orchard, two dams, paddocks for horses and cows, and masses of natural bushland. It was incredible: a dream life for a child and something I look back upon romantically. Some aspects, however, were difficult to enjoy, and they mainly had to do with work: more specifically working on the orchard.

My brother Mark and I must have been the only kids who didn't look forward with enormous gusto to the school summer holidays, simply because it meant a great deal of work for our parents and consequently less free time for the two of us. Don't get me wrong, we still managed to play cricket for our local team, Roleystone, on the weekend, watch Lillee and Marsh on the box whenever the sun burnt a hole in the sky, play cricket using an apple or pear as the ball and a hefty stick for a makeshift bat (that's just what us kids did), listen to cricket on the radio whenever there was a test match, and on one occasion go all that way to the WACA.

With the property came an archaic irrigation system, with the tiniest plastic taps, two of which were under most trees on the orchard. It was our job to crawl, kneel or bend under each of the trees and adjust the meagre amount of water trickling through these tiny plastic pipes, so the tall wilting sods got a sip on those dry, endless summer days. This is not such a fond memory: hours and hours of tweaking. We'd end up back at the beginning completely shattered and it looked to us as if we'd achieved nothing. A bit like painting the Harbour Bridge with a worn-out toothbrush. The water had a mind of its own and the irrigation system was a prick of a thing.

We had other chores over the seasons: cutting grass for the horses, picking mountains of fruit and collecting pruned branches and long twigs (occasionally used for the odd disciplinary measure), but nothing was quite as daunting as ten acres of trickle and we'd try absolutely anything to avoid that brutal job.

My brother mastered the art of sleeping in: a savvy move on his part. Funnily, though, napping till midday didn't quite cut it with our father. Poor Mum would step in on occasions to defend her growing eldest boy.

On those working days when the cricket wasn't on, I'd hear music drifting across the valley from Dad's radio, often tuned in to a golden hits station and I've no doubt it's somehow seeped into my psyche. Elvis, Roy Orbison, Neil Sedaka, Ricky Nelson, Connie Francis, '60s girl groups, Dusty Springfield, Ray Charles, Frank and Nancy Sinatra, Lee Hazelwood, The Beatles, The Stones and The Beach Boys – it's all swirling madly about this coconut of mine like a well-shaken daiquiri.

YOU'RE NOT ROB SNARSKI

Johnny Cash

For a time in the '90s, The Blackeyed Susans had some interest in the United States. *All Souls Alive* was licensed to the LA Punk Label Frontier Records, and *Mouth to Mouth* to Rick Rubin's American Recordings: home to Johnny Cash, The Black Crowes, The Jayhawks and The Jesus and Mary Chain, amongst others. It was a prestigious label, and to be label mates with Johnny Cash was, in my book, honourable.

When the opportunity to join the great southern gentleman at the CMJ music seminar in New York was presented to us, the sense of excitement washed over me like the parting of the Red Sea. This would be the first time we were to play outside of Australia, sharing the bill with Johnny Cash and June Carter, alt-country masters Wilco and the lesser known Parlour Jane. How did this happen? Who's throwing the dice here? Can my friends and family come?

So off we went with all our gear and a tour of the East Coast in place - Boston, Delaware, Hoboken, Detroit, Chicago, further north into Canada and back.

I'd been to NYC before, but never to perform; this was a first. I was staying in a photographer's apartment around Washington Square with our drummer Mark Dawson, and the others were Midtown in a hotel.

Things just happen in New York that don't seem to happen anywhere else. Phil Kakulas greeting Lou Reed in Greenwich Village, Dan being mugged, Kiernan Box losing his clothes, our van being towed away by the New York City Sheriff's Department, Mark Dawson being serenaded by a Mexican mariachi trumpeter. One night we were in Little Italy in a small bar which I vaguely remember being called something like Frank's Nuthouse. There in the corner was a vintage jukebox. Dan dropped in a coin and selected Santo & Johnny's ghostly instrumental *Sleep Walk*; the otherworldly sounds of the sparse, lonesome steel guitars filled the small room. Moments later we all piled into a black stretch limousine (at our own expense, as suggested by our travelling stagehand Jason Evans) and were subsequently driven over the Brooklyn Bridge. The strains of KISS playing a live outdoor concert somewhere out there amongst the mayhem drifted through on the warm night air. Things were getting surreal.

Being part of CMJ gave us the opportunity to witness some incredible music – Gillian Welch and Dave Rawlings, Junior Brown, The Friends of Dean Martinez, Lambchop, The Make-Up – as bands from around the globe congregated in New York for a week or two.

We rehearsed at a space called Rocket then had a bite to eat with our American label manager, Troy Hansborough, and our Australian MDS/Hi-Gloss rep, Simon Killen, in TriBeCa. Troy had unfortunate news that Johnny Cash was quite unwell, so the show had been arranged in a way that JC could finish up early; consequently, we would play directly before him and Wilco would now be finishing off the night.

The gig was at The Irving Plaza, a ballroom-style venue in the Union Square neighbourhood of Manhattan. Talking Heads and The Ramones had played there years before, The Clash and The B52s too, amongst others.

Our equipment was loaded in and we were waiting to sound-check. My first sight of JC was of him being supported either side by two of his bandmates, his strength sapped momentarily. A private moment that was difficult to watch; sad to see him struggling with his health.

Our own show flew by, lost in a slipstream of anxiety and a nervous energy. Apparently, when we performed *Smokin' Johnny Cash*, the man in black was at the side of the stage, looking on with his fellow musicians.

After our performance he wandered past our band room and looked in, our eyes met. I just couldn't bring myself to go upstairs to his band room like the other Susans to introduce myself until it was way too late. Fear of that awkward, unintelligible conversation; perhaps I'd stammer and say something completely inane. So, in a way, I was quietly relieved and only a little saddened when Jeff Tweedy told me they'd locked the door by the time I'd managed to muster the courage to wander up the stairs myself.

Dan and Phil didn't hold back. Phil had introduced himself, shaken his hand, and, graciously, Johnny Cash had thanked him for the song in a thick, charming southern drawl. He'd signed a few things and wished the band luck.

I watched Johnny Cash and June Carter sing their way through a set of old and new. June played autoharp for an old Carter Family tune, they duetted on 'Jackson', the keyboardist found a trumpet-like sound to emulate the brass on 'Ring of Fire'. I stood there at the back of the room listening to his powerful, aged, majestic voice: forging ahead, difficult to decipher he was so unwell, and every so often June would carry their show.

I found myself simply wishing my family could've been there to share the experience.

Birth

When I was a child, my father would tease me when the moment suited. He'd be half-smirking, telling me I was adopted. I reacted by running off crying into my room, a little confused by this possibility. I had a darker complexion than my brother, similar to my mother's olive skin, and the kids at school nicknamed me everything from *Eski* (as in Inuit) to *Cochise* (as in Apache), not quite knowing what to make of me. I would turn a deepish brown after my first summer swim.

My poor mother would reprimand my father and then again have to retell the story of my birth. My father was always the tormentor/comedian, and my mother the mediator and troubleshooter.

I was born at the family home in South Ealing, London. The choice was my mother's. Her hospital experience when giving birth to my older brother Mark had been so unpleasant that she decided on a home birth for me. I'd be born with a midwife to deliver, simple. She'd been shopping that afternoon and felt her first contractions begin that evening whilst she was relaxing after sorting out her fruit and veg. It had been a beautiful day in Ealing – blue skies, sun shining – and Mark had been well-behaved. She rang her doctor, then the midwife rang her. My father then hopped in the car and picked up Babcia from neighbouring Hanwell. There was only a small family audience for my emergence. I popped out later into the night at about 10.30pm, with no pain relief for my mother. She just clutched on to the pillows and held on to my father's hand as Babcia watched on anxiously, desperately hoping for her first granddaughter. I didn't wail or scream when I arrived, apparently, so the midwife gave me the standard sharp slap on the butt in order for me to take my first gasp.

My mother had a harrowing childhood. The Soviets had invaded Eastern Poland just after Christmas; she was four years old and her family were taken by train to a labour camp in Siberia. Prior to that, her father had been forced to leave; news travelled fast and the townsfolk had been told that the men were being taken away and killed. So the family had a long journey to Siberia without their father. Mum's youngest sister died through lack of food and the harsh conditions, so my grandmother single-handedly buried her own child in the snow by a train platform. She dug a shallow grave and covered her daughter's frail body by hand. The siblings huddled together and watched on from the train carriage, not quite comprehending what had happened.

Most days in the labour camp my grandmother received a meagre portion of bread for the family to survive on. My mother and her older brother Richard would find cow dung in the nearby forests and forage through it to find edible seeds or nuts. There was simply not enough food. Sometimes when there was nothing at all, they would eat snow.

Armadale, 1967.

Chad's Tree

My parents bought a house in Kelmscott in my last year of high school, sold their beloved orchard and land in Karragullen to move to a half-acre block in the south-eastern suburbs of Perth. The physical nature of orchard work and the isolation were taking their toll; we also wanted to be closer to our friends. Dad decided to buy a fish and chip shop, unbeknownst to my mother.

The new house stood across the road from a paddock where horses and cows roamed amongst towering power lines. At one end of the street was a salt lake and caravan park, and at the other a bus depot. All the houses in the street seemed to be scarred by the same yellow-rusty-brown bore-water stains.

Our mother, being a biology teacher, loved to have an array of animals around her. Most afternoons I'd arrive home to find either peacocks on the roof or geese in the swimming pool. We had a pink and grey galah that accurately mimicked the sound of a dog's bark and managed a faultless impersonation of my mother's call that dinner was ready, replete with Polish accent. Mum also kept axolotls in a fish tank in the dining room, which she would hand-feed raw bits of meat around dinnertime, one an albino with piercing red eyes. I found them a little creepy but my mother was fascinated by the fact their limbs would regenerate if damaged or bitten off by one of the others, perhaps half-studying them.

Kelmscott Shopping Centre went up in flames around that year. One of the kids from school set it alight, apparently. Kelmscott wasn't dissimilar to other suburbs out there, home of the first ever Red Rooster outlet in Australia.

My brother had a large bedroom to the side of the house. A young man cave, with a bar and a serious stereo. Fellow musicians often complained of the distance to get here; the 23 kilometres from town was just a bit too taxing. Still this is where Chad's Tree initially rehearsed.

After seeing numerous original bands in Perth at The Shaftsbury, The Cat, The Broadway, Adrian's, The Wizbah and The Red Parrot, and tuning in to The Velvets, The Doors and Television, my brother Mark had started writing songs.

I'd met our new drummer, James Hurst, through his younger brother and my work colleague Jonathon. James was innovative and interesting, he pushed the songs' arrangements, had a deep 12" marching snare and never opted to play obvious straight 4/4 or 3/4 rhythms. He was also drummer in a band called The IDs (Inept Dilettantes) who often supported The Triffids, mixing up surf instrumentals and Jonathan Richman covers with a splash of The Velvets.

James loved Ringo, but would never admit it publicly; rarely would he let it slip that the Beatle had taught him a thing or two (he could potentially have me bumped off for mentioning this). We juggled bass players for a time, Mark Hemery, a budding state hockey player and law student, and then Peter Michael (son of the Lord Mayor).

Chad's Tree played a lot of shows in Perth at all the venues we'd frequent to see local original bands – Stray Tapes, AndAnA,

The Manikins, The Scientists, German Humour, The Triffids, Rhythm Method, The Wanderlust Trio, The Helicopters, along with touring bands from interstate and overseas.

After a couple of years we were coaxed by our musician friends to head off to the Eastern States. It was time to move on and try our luck closer to record labels and studios. We left behind the vast blue skies, the intense light of day, the long, hot sweltering summers, friends and family, our beloved 'State of Excitement', and found ourselves in a dilapidated terrace house in Erskineville on the aptly named Morrissey Road. It was 1986.

Kelmscott, 1982.

Roleystone Pool

The neighbours' kid, Robert Wood, was quite the scoundrel; he was also my best friend. He convinced me it was a brilliant idea to bury my toys; only problem was we usually forgot where they were exactly, much to my parents' disbelief and frustration. We painted the walls with our pastel interpretation of Casper the Friendly Ghost lost in a forest, and turned the bedroom into teepees and a Cowboys and Indians battleground on occasion, the usual kid stuff.

The Woods had a tree house, made of hessian bags, way up high in a gum tree, which we were only allowed in rarely, as it was the domain of older brother Michael. The floor felt wrong to me, loose and unsafe. We'd walk precariously along the sagging hessian floor half-expecting our legs to fall through. So instead Robert and I chose to climb onto the corrugated roof of a large shed behind our house, where we'd eat copious amounts of loquats from the tree that grew alongside. We'd climb the loquat tree to get to the top of the shed and feast upon the sweet, delicious fruit. I remember slipping, falling and sliding down the slanted corrugated tin, thinking I was about to fall to my peril, break all my bones and subsequently die. Suddenly Robert's hand came out of nowhere and pulled me to safety. We were as thick as thieves, as any five-year-olds could be. No school at this point, just lots and lots of time.

Summers could be unbearable in Armadale; the heat was unrelenting and the blustery dry easterlies were sapping. My parents had just about had enough on one of those sweltering summer days and decided to take us all for a drive and a dip to Roleystone Pool, a large natural swimming hole, hidden up in the hills. Robert Wood was coming along too and he brought a big, black, blown-up tractor-tyre tube – at this point we still hadn't learnt to swim. We all piled into the Holden: folks up the front, kids in the back.

The 'pool' was heaving. Dad found a spot for the family to spread out and where he and Mum could look out over the noisy expanse of water. My father was exhausted from a long run of night shifts and managed to fall asleep almost instantly amongst the mayhem. There was quite a gathering; everyone from around the area seemed to have the same idea. Kids splashing, dogs barking, families enjoying a moment's respite from the unbearable heat.

My brother Mark and Robert Wood had taken off on the magical rubber tube. I could see them on the far side of the water, splashing about where the pool was slightly less crowded. They were floating and paddling around slowly, having far too much fun for what seemed like far too long. I started feeling anxious, jealous, left out, a tantrum was brewing. I began wandering through the water towards them, my feet feeling their way through the murky soft muddy floor. Then the level suddenly dropped and I began sinking into a deep dip several metres to the bottom. I could see through the water the red glow of the sun way up high, directly above me, and could hear the muffled screams of my mother as she threw herself in.

The only problem was my mother couldn't swim either and consequently struggled after she'd grabbed a hold of me.

Within seconds a bearded stranger dived in and saved both of us: a Herculean effort. I was slung over his shoulder as he hoisted us both out. I remember throwing up copious amounts of water, gasping for air, then thinking about the red sun way up high…*surely it was now my turn for the magical rubber tube?*

The Triffids

There is no doubt I saw The Triffids more than any other band from my youth. There was a time I'd see every show when they returned to WA from the Eastern States, and also in Sydney (where I'd relocated with Chad's Tree) whenever they returned home from Europe for an Australian tour.

I wasn't an early attendee; I don't even remember seeing them at The Stoned Crow. I didn't have the original Tapes 1, 2, 3 or 4, 5, 6 and I've only recently been able to find my copy of *Dungeon Tape* (the handwriting on the cassette unmistakably David McComb's). The first time I saw and heard them was at The Cat and Fiddle Tavern on Beaufort Street in Mt Lawley, now The Flying Scotsman & Velvet Lounge. Back in the day this place seemed to be a haven for the misfits of the subcultures that existed in Perth at the time - skinheads, punks, mods, the occasional rockabilly and fashionista. The crowd appeared to be part Quadrophenia, part aspiring musician and a curious mixture of folk interested in our *'alternative music scene'*. Cover bands reigned supreme in Perth; there were only a handful of venues scattered about to see and hear original music and even then original bands would slip in a cover or two.

The Cat was the first place I saw Tony Thewlis, from The Scientists play guitar with our friends' band The Helicopters. Brian Hooper, prior to The Beasts of Bourbon, impressed with what sounded like a note-perfect cover of *Public Image* in one of his guises on that little stage at the back of that long, darkly lit room.

I wasn't sure what to expect of The Triffids on that bright Sunday afternoon. I'd only read a little bit about them in the street rags and fanzines of the day. They appeared less consumed by fashion and the subcultures on display than other bands and looked relatively unassuming. There were more chequered shirts than tablecloths in a Polish restaurant and no feigned bravado or posturing. They struck me as being outsiders, with a sense of not really belonging or wanting to, comfortable doing their own thing - original, more alternative than the alternatives, more NY than UK. I was curious.

David McComb, Shaftsbury Hotel, Perth 1982.

Lambsie

It's easy to imagine my grandmother as a busy, young Polish farm girl. When I was a kid she was often collecting eggs or plucking feathers from freshly slain chooks or making her own cheese: bags of curdling milk suspended around the veranda with bits of murky white liquid dripping into trays below.

She and my grandfather emigrated to Australia in the early 1970s after a time in the UK. My grandfather had served as a paramilitary trooper for the Polish army in WWII, whilst Babcia had brought up her two sons in the Koja Polish refugee camp on the banks of Lake Victoria in Uganda. They had spent some time in a Siberian labour camp before eventually making their way to Africa.

She was a big lass who loved to cook, to eat and to feed the family. I remember sitting on her knee on occasions as she peeled and fed me apples and raw dough before baking a pie or two. The ravages of the war had taken its toll on my folks and grandparents. Food was essential. We had to be fed, we could never be without, and the portions were never meagre. Food was simply everywhere on the farm, we were surrounded by food growing, and animals wandering amongst the paddocks. I must have been around five or six when I saw my first chicken headed for the chopping block: startled by it running about headless, with plumes of blood spurting out from its neck. I didn't know what was happening, it was almost cartoon-like. There were always animals coming and going, it seemed: geese, cows, pigs ... sheep.

Lambsie had been rejected by her mother and brought to us by the neighbours. Such a sweet, lovely beast – so white and fluffy, every little kid's dream. She was affectionate, adorable and playful. Our very own living, breathing, woolly toy.

We had a wide gravel driveway that ran 100 metres from the road to the house. Every afternoon coming home from school, as we drove the final length, Lambsie would race up to the gate and then skip along by the side of the car *baaaah*-ing excitedly – our precious fluffy cloud – eager to see us and receive a cuddle or two. She was in search of her flock, an only sheep, and we were the closest thing to siblings.

One afternoon, when Lambsie didn't appear by the gate, we three experienced a simultaneous stab of panic. There we were, arriving in the car, at the gate: same time, same routine, straight after school and no fluffy white cloud to greet us. We rolled slowly along the gravel, the wheels dragging us home, all of us keeping a keen eye out for our four-legged friend. We looked past the plum and pear trees, towards the dam and out across the paddocks but, alas, no Lambsie to be seen.

We finally rolled up to the house, pulling up under the massive grapevine where the car was partially shaded from the heat. We looked slightly further out, away from the house, and there we saw my father and Babcia busy attending to something. To our utter horror Lambsie was dangling from the clothes line, partially skinned, throat cut with her deep red blood draining down into a bucket below. A shocking, harrowing sight and it didn't take long to comprehend exactly what was going on. We burst into tears as Mum quickly leapt out from the car. Then there was a harsh exchange in Polish between Babcia, Mum and my father. We were told by my mother to go inside. I felt a heaviness in my belly: hollow, confused, betrayed and sick to the core.

Hours passed and the house was still. No-one seemed to want to talk; there was an uncomfortable, cold atmosphere. We were summoned to the dinner table some hours later, where our meals were waiting. There on the plate were small unrecognisable parts of our beloved Lambsie. This can't be right. I refused to eat. Mark refused to eat. My father was certainly not going to be beaten by his two sons' silent protest. He simply bellowed in a demanding tone, 'Eat it!' …and we did … slowly, reluctantly and resentfully. Tears dripped onto the plate and onto the flesh in front of me. It was a salty, bitter-tasting meal, eaten in complete silence apart from our occasional sobs.

The Go-Betweens

In 1983 The Go-Betweens toured WA for the first time and for some reason their rather generous promoter, Neil Wedd, decided to have Chad's Tree support them at each of their four shows. I'm not sure that happened much in those days but I can assure you that I was ecstatic and partially overwhelmed by this prospect. Their album *Send Me A Lullaby* was in amongst my record collection, and now they were touring to promote their new release 'Before Hollywood' with its leading track, 'Cattle and Cane', earning them much-deserved attention and radio play. In fact, I remember the exact moment I heard that particular song bouncing off the wooden floors of a share house in Subiaco. Grant McLennan was being interviewed on 6UVS and the song had recently been tagged as 'quintessentially Australian'; Grant simply agreed.

The sound of it swept me away. Bass notes doubling a lonesome acoustic guitar, circling and ringing out before a soft wave of reverb washed over. Persistent high hats and driving bass drum, interweaving guitar parts accompanying the quietest of singing and nestling a lyric brimming with childhood memories and raw sentiment. For me it was an incredible musical moment, similar in a way to when I first heard Television's 'See No Evil' or in later years Arvo Pärt's 'Spiegel Im Spiegel'. Time moved in a mysterious way, slow-mo, a mesmerising sonic spell.

The Go-Betweens themselves were, to my surprise, friendly and outgoing, quite the gregarious bunch, the flipside to what I'd been expecting. Lindy was lovely, chatty and vivacious. Robert Forster mentioned they'd just come from Melbourne, where they'd played with a remarkable band he had fallen for – The Moodists. Rob Vickers played so many bass notes it was impossible to keep count. He also looked years below his true age, a schoolboy Brian Jones who'd run off to join the circus. Grant proudly wore a white Sergeant Pepper's military-style jacket on stage. To me, these eccentric Brisbane musician folk

The Go-Betweens, Red Parrot, Perth 1983.

and literary aficionados were exotic creatures. 'Have you read *Le Grande Meaulnes*? You must.'

Perth audiences were in awe of them, listening pensively. Some sitting and sticking to the floral carpet of The Apollo Room.

I saw them play live quite a lot over the coming years and with various line-ups. In 1986 violinist Amanda Brown had joined and by this point in time Chad's Tree had moved to Sydney. Amanda graciously accompanied us for a show or two and guested on our debut album *Buckle in the Rail*.

The last time I saw Grant, though, was one afternoon at Ric's Bar in Fortitude Valley, 2002. Long Island Iced Tea was his drink of choice on this sultry Brisbane day. I was playing a lazy afternoon gig there with Dan Luscombe, a little side show of ours as we toured the country as guests of Augie March. Grant was in good spirits, cheerful and enthusiastic. He commented on how much he loved one particular song we'd played: a new tune called 'Henry Small'. It sounded to him as if it was from a distant era ... another time and another place.

The Accordion

Babcia – my grandmother - loved music and as a young girl she played the balalaika. She enjoyed more contemporary western music too, even had a soft spot for John Paul Young back in the day and regularly watched *Countdown* with us on a Sunday night. It had become a ritual – Molly Meldrum, Babcia and her two grandsons. Her favourite song was Joe Dolce's 'Shaddup You Face' and still, to this day, it manages to worm its way out from my memory banks. I find myself humming the melody, shuffling my feet and having to consciously force myself to stop.

At one point in the late '70s, Babcia seriously considered having me chaperone her to a Rod Stewart concert at the Perth Entertainment Centre. Now, that really would've been quite a sight and experience but unfortunately the idea slipped through the net.

Before all of this, she had decided that we should be more musical, we should both learn a musical instrument – she had, so we must – simple.

One day, without any consultation that I can recall, a classical guitar and an accordion appeared in the house. Being the youngest, I had second choice: I was given the accordion as Mark had less than zero interest in this strange antediluvian contraption, with its large wheezing bellows and myriad keys and buttons.

I'd be driven by our mother to my music teacher Keith Saw's house, somewhere off the steepest of hills on Echo Road in Kelmscott, once a week after school. I was taught scales for the right hand and the bass lines on the left to accompany the melodies and then eventually songs. I was supremely dedicated (sort of). Essentially I'd practise during a current affairs program or in between homework. Back in my school days I could quite easily watch five hours of television uninterrupted (which, to be honest, hasn't changed all that much) but I could easily tear myself away from current news items, a lot easier than from, *Get Smart* or *Lost In Space* to practise my beloved squeezebox.

It was tough going for a tubby Polish kid; expectations were high. Every so often my folks or Babcia would drag me out in front of some ancient-looking visitors to perform a song or two.

'Do I have to …?' Yes, I had to. It was only mildly excruciating; more excruciating were eisteddfods where I had to compete with other young kids in front of a panel of judges. I was, quite frankly, hopeless. My anxiety levels won on every occasion and I would perform the tunes at twice the speed, with twice as many mistakes and with about as much feel as a dull blade of grass. I stared at the pages as the musical dots began to merge on the music stand before me. I'd have practised the piece endlessly; it would be memorised, stored up there somewhere between my ears. I would have played the songs perfectly at home, over and over again and also during lessons, but as soon as there was an audience or a stage, I just took flight and whipped through the tunes like I needed to be somewhere two weeks ago. But my folks and Babcia persisted; they thought it was important, eventually it would work out.

My accordion was a beautiful deep red-coloured Paolo Soprani, with a glorious warm tone; the body glistened and sparkled with bits of mother-of-pearl. It was like a wonderful old automobile and just as heavy; there were 120 bass buttons – a lot. I played for several years, entered and lost numerous eisteddfods. I tried to learn songs from the radio, and got to be pretty good melodically, as far as twelve-year-old piano accordion players went.

When presented with the music for the 'William Tell Overture' during one of the school summer breaks, I decided that was about all I could take; the well had run dry. Rossini and The Lone Ranger teamed up and shot me down. 'Bugs Bunny's Overtures to Disaster' was indeed my own disaster and my ultimate finale.

So, head hung low, I told my folks I had simply lost interest in playing the instrument. It was getting too difficult, taking up far too much time; high school loomed large and my polka-playing days were over. I wasn't sure playing piano accordion in high school was all that cool. Potentially a kid could get beaten up for divulging something like that at Kelmscott Senior High, I'd imagined. Trying to soften the blow, I suggested maybe I could learn guitar instead. Not really what my ma and pa wanted to hear: three years of wasted lessons, words reverberating around the house, what a great shame.

By this time I was more interested in contemporary songs on the radio and would sing everything that came out of those tiny car speakers, much to my brother's annoyance. Each morning and afternoon on our school drive I'd be warbling

THE ACCORDION

away in the front passenger seat, Mum weaving up and down the Brookton Highway in the Holden, dragging away on the occasional Escort.

'Will you SHUT UP!' was the standard response from my brother a few feet behind me. He'd heard enough and was reaching boiling point. Alas, there was no respite from this new form of musical hell.

Under 14s Football

'Hit him, Robert, hit him!' my father was yelling in his big, booming voice, sounding a little panicked. He was parked on the perimeter of the footy oval and had by this stage emerged from the car.

I was standing on a half back flank in my Roleystone guernsey and some kid from the rival team, Armadale, had just booted me firmly in the shin. I then pushed him hard in the chest in retaliation and moved on. This simply wasn't enough, apparently. My dad's yelling persisted, with the occasional car honk thrown in. Roleystone lost pretty much every week by about ten to fifteen goals, and I often played full back, was kept busy kicking out from goal or attempting to spoil the much faster leading forwards.

The quarter-time siren sounded and my father summonsed me to the boundary line, where I copped quite a serve. Something along the lines of: *If I didn't deck that kid by game's end my football days were over, no more training, no more this, no more that ... and I certainly wouldn't be getting a lift home.*

Dad was a hefty guy, twenty odd stone in the old scale. He had previously been on this very oval at training, challenging the kids to tackle him. Groups of them ran up and jumped at my father, the man-mountain, and he simply brushed them off like specks of dirt in a Hulk-like manner.

I'd realised early on that I was not a fighting guy, my heart just wasn't in it. I'd once had a fight at primary school and beaten this kid up – Joel something. Anyway, he cried so much, I then cried. I'm not sure who cried more in the end, but my desk turned into a puddle of tears and so did his. I guessed it just wasn't me. My brother, on the other hand, would fight. He wasn't shy about throwing a punch or two, and nursed the occasional bruise or blood nose. He'd often get into a scrap with the next-door neighbour or some other kid at school. I remember being horrified at seeing blood running down his face after one of his efforts on the oval at recess.

This was going to be a long, long day, the match was one-sided. Were we twelve goals down? I sensed my adversary was regretting his actions and I was wondering how on earth I was going to deal with this situation. Maybe the world would be overrun by aliens by the final siren. I pushed him around a bit but couldn't do the biffing part. The game ended in another massive defeat for our side. We were a small community on the outskirts of the metropolitan area, with barely enough kids to field a side. It felt as if everyone had been watching.

I was feeling pretty low. Head down, I gathered my belongings from the change rooms and wandered slowly up to the car where my father was waiting a little impatiently. Not happy. The sense of fury was evident from his reddened face and half-bulging eyes. Frankly, I was petrified; he was ropeable and felt terribly embarrassed. I sat in the front seat of our orange Holden HR station wagon as he drove away in silence; I sensed he was ashamed to be my dad. Occasionally the silence was split by a barrage of caustic words, alternating with a spit out the window and a drag on his rollie. I wondered why I couldn't punch this other kid, retaliate, and defend myself to another level. All I wanted to do was switch on the car radio and lose myself in some music.

Susie the Bush Kangaroo

The students from Armadale High (where my mother taught and was Head of the Science Department) would on occasion bring in an injured animal for her to appraise. Mum's copious passion for life and for all creatures great and small was evident in her Biology class.

On one occasion an echidna was rummaging about in a cardboard box on the back seat of our car as we drove home from school. After Mum somehow examined the spiky beast, it wandered off into the vast acres of bushland on our property in search of a new home.

We received a phone call late one night from one of Mum's ex-students. The boy had been 'roo shooting somewhere on the outskirts of Perth and had discovered a joey tucked away in the pouch of one of his victims. Mum cared for the poor orphan – all floppy limbs and lengthy tail – and it would sleep in a fur-lined winter-coat, now redesigned as a pouch and hung on the back of my brother's bedroom door. Eventually, Susie made her way onto Mark's bed and he'd wake up to find little dark round Easter egg–like droppings distributed upon his bedding, with the squiggly animal standing over him each morning *tt-tt-tt*-ing.

Susie recovered well and grew strong. She stayed on our property for our remaining time in Karragullen. Initially she hung out with Poochie, the loyal border collie, until she felt comfortable enough to bound about the orchard and the surroundings all by herself. There was every opportunity for her to leave but she chose to stay close to our family, this beautiful and most gentle of creatures. She'd follow us around the orchard or come to the house when she heard us pull up in the driveway and we'd feed her toast or bits of chocolate. On one occasion the local baker accidentally ran over her tail and my father managed to bandage it up with two splints either side; she had a little bend in her rudder from that moment on.

One afternoon, Babcia carelessly tied her up next to our vegetable patch. We arrived home from school that day, horrified to find her head puffed out and swollen, like a little furry balloon with ears; Mum quickly loosened the knot. Not the sharpest blade in the drawer, our Babcia. There was a mix of Polish profanities and Polish tears when my father arrived on the scene. Poor Babica, poor kangaroo.

Susie bounded down the driveway one afternoon to show off her new handsome companion: a big grey. She stopped by swiftly to greet us and then hopped away, joining him in the top paddock. It was the first time we'd seen her with an admirer, such a beautiful and majestic sight.

Babcia suggested bringing Susie (and the remaining pigs) to our new suburban dwelling in Kelmscott but we all knew her home was up there. Occasionally there was news about her from the neighbours. Eventually she was killed, being chased by their dogs, her neck broken whilst trying to escape under a high gate, carrying a joey for the first time.

The Fonz

There was a time in my teenage life, when all we seemed to do for entertainment on a Saturday night was drive around town watching people and checking out cars. We'd often grab something to eat late at night on our way home. My parents asked my brother to let me tag along so they could have a break from the pair of us. Consequently, Mark had to put up with me hanging around, cramping his style, being a young, annoying, sibling pest. Occasionally we'd go to the drive-in, where I'd hide in the boot of the car and not have to pay the entry fee. We'd bump into Mark's school pals, some who had panel vans and girlfriends.

The birds and bees talk didn't go so well with my folks; somehow it turned into roosters, hens and eggs. My brother walked in and simply said, 'I'll tell you about it later.'

After one of our late-night excursions, we found ourselves sitting in a booth at a burger joint in Gosnells with my brother's best pal, Eddie. Eddie was a great guy: smart, good-natured, sensible. We were looking out the window at the various cars turning up, their owners and girlfriends. Holdens, Falcons, Toranas, Monaros, whatever... I didn't know much about hot cars or hot girls and I still don't.

The standard dress for a suburban teenager back in the day was a simple black t-shirt, Levi jeans and ripple sole desert boots. The music of choice blaring from the car cassette was typically AC/DC or KISS, occasionally Led Zeppelin, Neil Young, Suzi Quatro, The Sweet or Bowie.

At some point, halfway through our burgers and chips, a loner guy found himself in the car park being confronted by about half-a-dozen long-haired, intimidating-looking dudes. This guy stood his ground as we watched on from inside. It was turning pretty ugly out there and the tension was palpable: far too much testosterone going on. I froze in my seat, Eddie too, but my brother leapt from the booth without a word and headed out the door. He's like that, my brother, not scared to lend a fist in an uneven contest. He stood in between the antagonists and this poor guy, warning the gang to leave the complete stranger be or take him on too. Jesus Christ, what the hell!

The tension slowly dissipated. The youths meandered back to their respective cars and girlfriends. The innocent loner guy quietly thanked Mark and proceeded to wander off into the night.

My brother had somehow morphed into Arthur Fonzarelli.

Eddie and I looked at each other with complete disbelief. Who does that?

Mark in Madrid, 1990.

The Reels

From memory, when I first saw The Reels on *Countdown* I'm pretty sure there wasn't a conventional guitar in sight, which was unusual for an Australian band in 1979. They looked a little androgynous; maybe there was a woman in the band – combining that with coming from Dubbo, rural New South Wales, well, that was impressive enough in itself. Now, were they playing 'Love Will Find a Way' or 'Prefab Heart'?

I saw them perform live at a sold-out gig in WA sometime later, around 1982. I was one of the unsuspecting members of the audience that Dave Mason wandered up to. He thrust the microphone in my face to say something vitally important for the whole gathering at Curtin University to hear. Well, that was never going to happen. I mumbled something about 'peace', I think.

Years later, whilst living in Sydney, I formed a musical trio with Sue Grigg and Kenny Davis Jnr, jangling away playing Dylan, Cohen, plus a country ballad or two. So how our naïve little trio, known as Three Strange Loves ended up supporting The Reels at the Sydney Cove Tavern is a complete and utter mystery. They were kind to us bumbling youngsters, though, suggesting varying the keys of songs to give the overall set a little more variety. Ah, E minor, the saddest of keys.

In London in 1989, I was working with David McComb and Kenny Davis Jnr on an EP for The Blackeyed Susans called *Depends On What You Mean by Love* a late-night record, plaintive, sombre. There are reference points to The Reels' album *Beautiful*; their reworking of classic ballads from Bacharach to Humperdinck were McComb's favourites.

A decade on and I record 'Quasimodo's Dream' twice; firstly with a 3RRR band for a live release called RRRewind in the Chapel in 1999, and again for The Blackeyed Susans' *Dedicated to the Ones We Love* in 2001 ... such a mysterious, sad song.

Throw to 2008 and I'm solo support to The Reels at Don't Tell Tom, a bar on Sydney Road, Brunswick. They'd re-formed for a short tour. My partner Peter was mortified to overhear a woman gasp at the bar when she saw me wander onto the stage: 'Oh dear, he hasn't aged well, has he? He looks like Mr Potato Head.' Charming, thank you.

The comedian Dave O'Neil happened to be seated at the front table with some other folk eager to see and hear The Reels. Luckily I didn't have to play for too long as there was a heavy air of anticipation and polite impatience from the full house gathering there. I got through my set as swiftly as I could, packed up my guitar and made my way to the bar to settle my nerves.

The folk who came along knew all the songs and were very appreciative, as Dave's fragile, wonderful voice floated above us all. Then, mid-song, towards the end of their set – perhaps during 'This Guy's in Love' – Dave Mason again wanders through the crowd with mic in hand, singing away, and catches sight of me standing at the edge of the dance floor.

He's mouthing something at me ...*What's he doing?* Suddenly I'm feeling slightly awkward, embarrassed and a little self-conscious. Now he's making his way through the audience, determined, heading in my direction. He's mouthing 'I've got your pay,' and wanders straight up to me and sticks a few crisp notes in my top pocket. Uh-huh, well, that's slightly unconventional.

More recently I shared the stage again with Dave Mason, along with Sean Kelly from The Models and Brendan Gallagher from Karma County, at MEMO in St Kilda. I remember wondering before the gig what mischievous antics Dave may conjure up on the evening... thankfully none that involved me.

Laughing Clowns

Chad's Tree supported The Laughing Clowns in Perth once, possibly twice, at the Wizbah and then at the Shenton Park Hotel; from memory it was sometime around 1984. They were a remarkable band - part jazz, part punk, part noise, with interesting time signatures and inimitable melodies. Ed Kuepper, their singer/writer/guitarist, was someone my brother Mark and I were pretty much in awe of.

On the first night, Mark had been 'plying himself with a little Dutch courage, preparing to introduce himself to our musical hero as I watched on in the shadows, finding it all too overwhelming. A friend of ours, Mark Beyer, had introduced us to the music of The Saints and in relatively recent times we'd moved on to The Laughing Clowns. Ed was also held in high regard amongst our circle of musician friends, legendary in fact.

So at night's end we found ourselves in the band room with Ed and his bandmates. My brother by this stage was quite, though not quietly, plastered. If there was a trophy for drinking copious amounts of booze before meeting someone you admire, my brother would have a few lined up side by side on his mantelpiece, alongside his cricket trophy.

Mark leant across with an extended hand, looking like a Dickensian hustler, dressed in an op-shop jacket and waistcoat, with a fob watch and chain dangling from his pocket and buckles on his black leather shoes. He slurred something like 'Mr Kuepper, it's an honour to meet you.'

Ed, a little agitated, responded with 'Would you mind removing your foot from my guitar case?' Well, things were going swimmingly, Mark half-standing on Ed's fender Stratocaster case; I have no idea how, well, I do, actually – he was hammered.

The following night at the Shenton Park Hotel their lighting guy, Doug Wade, asked if our band was named after Chad Morgan, the charming big-toothed Australian country singer. Their trombone player, Glad Reed, was lovely and friendly, ending up playing in Mark's future band The Jackson Code.

I didn't see Ed again until a year later, when Chad's Tree had relocated to Sydney. Bands had to do that in those days; you couldn't sign to a label and stay in Perth, there was no internet or Triple J, no social media, and plane fares were exorbitant. The Eastern States were the rainbow's end, a romantic place where all one's musical dreams would come true.

We happened to be in the Hot Records offices in Darlinghurst one afternoon, discussing our debut seven-inch vinyl release, *Crush the Lily*. I noticed Ed was there too in another of their offices, no doubt discussing his first solo offering *Electrical Storm*. So, here we are signing to the same label as The Laughing Clowns and The Triffids, and Ed Kuepper is here in the same building. It felt incredible, like we sort of belonged here in a bizarro, how-the-hell-did-this-happen kind of way ... this was really happening.

The following day I found myself wandering the streets of Newtown, the inner-west suburb of Sydney. I swear there was only one café on this stretch of King Street back in 1986, and it wasn't far from the only op shop for a mile or two. I'm meandering away, looking about shops and, lo and behold, who's heading in my direction? Yes, Ed himself. I can feel myself turning into *Fanboy*. I'm blushing and feeling like I should probably cross the street to avoid any clumsy confrontation, but I don't. Ed stops me, yes, that's right, Ed Kuepper stops me and asks, 'Aren't you in Chad's Tree?' Okay, this is ludicrous. Ed Kuepper is asking me if I'm in Chad's Tree... this simply cannot be real. I manage to mumble something, which may have been a word. He says he likes our drummer's unique approach, his deep-sounding snare, and is happy that we're going to be labelmates, and then he wanders off homebound. I, of course, am gobsmacked, stunned by this encounter with my musical demigod. Ed Kuepper asked me if I was in Chad's Tree...!

I think I must have told anyone and every fence post interested in this majestic encounter as I strolled back home to Erskineville. Ed Kuepper asked if I was in Chad's Tree... who's going to believe that?

That night I had the most surreal of dreams ... I was again walking along King Street. I could see something, an unfamiliar shape, way up ahead in the distance. I walked and walked until eventually I reached it. There it stood in front of me, a bronze statue, Atlas-like, glistening in the polluted sun ... it was Ed Kuepper.

Chad's Tree "Buckle In the Rail" BBQ - Morrissey Road, Erskineville.
David Nichols, Mark Snarski, Ed Kuepper, Mark Dawson, Louis Tillet.

David and Margaret

Margaret, a friend of ours, had started seeing Dave McComb and, after a time, tease-tortured me with the idea of bringing him along to the Shaftsbury Hotel to watch and hear Chad's Tree.

We'd played our debut show there only a few months before at an original band night, where entry was free before 8.30pm and one dollar for the unemployed with ID – not bad for three acts. On that particular night (our first public show) my nerves were so charged, the songs played themselves at what seemed like twice the speed and the set list was over almost as quickly as it had begun. I'd like to think our friends Julianna, Nikki and Margaret, and possibly Teresa, danced (which could only have been a good thing). From memory Matthew, Craig and Paul didn't bag us, in fact they were all quite complimentary. Overall positive, it went well, no-one self-combusted.

The Shaftsbury was on the Northbridge side of Perth, over the Horseshoe Bridge, across from the offices of the *West Australian* newspaper. A couple of doors down was a blues bar called The Loaded Dog (where our friend and guitar virtuoso friend Kim Bettenay often played) and around the corner was a small hipster club called The Silver Slipper. Oddly, it didn't really feel like it was a happening strip; if anything it felt like a relatively dark and secluded, quiet part of town.

Several months after our debut there we were playing with AndAnA. They took their cues from the likes of Kraftwerk and Pere Ubu —electric guitar, drum machine, synthesiser and screeching, manic vocals. Engaging, intense, creating an incredible racket for a three-piece.

'I hear the birdies go tweet tweet tweet tweet!' screeched David Kelsall, as if the four horsemen of the apocalypse were fast approaching over the Horseshoe Bridge, half-shoving the microphone down his throat. How this harsh, piercing sound emanated from such a slightly built and polite gent was beyond me. Tony Roncevic, their guitarist, often had a photograph or magazine cutting of a female nude clipped to his music stand alongside a picture of Elvis, a rather strange juxtaposition, I thought; or perhaps not.

Our set followed and when it was over, I remember Dave McComb poking his head around the corner into the band room, with a big-toothed grin, half-berating, half-complimenting us after hearing Chad's Tree for the first time.

'You Snarski brothers can sing like The Walker Brothers and play guitar like Television... utter bastards.' Great, he likes us.

I was living on Lawrence Avenue, West Perth, at the time, paying twenty-four dollars a week in rent. It was close to pretty much everything and I could walk into town to my dull day job in the public service.

I remember David and Margaret dropping over, I was sticking close to a bunch of my older records, playing DJ. 'Sitting on the Dock of the Bay', 'Here Comes the Night', 'Cathy's Clown', 'To Sir with Love': The Lighthouse Keepers, one of Dave's favourite bands in Sydney at the time, were playing the song as their encore, he enthused. I also remember Dave asking if buying an extra copy of Van Morrison's *Astral Weeks* and BigStar's *Third/Sister Lovers* was indulgent. He simply wanted to have one copy for Perth, and one for Sydney.

I'd read a list of his heroes in a fanzine a year before: Billie Holiday and Richard Hell among them. I remember assuming Billie Holiday was a guy.

David had also written an article about Melbourne band The Moodists in a fanzine, where he'd claimed the crown of James Osterburg was up for grabs; their lead singer Dave Graney held a tight grip on it, such were his stage antics and attitude, his snarling, smooth, panther-like croon, his flair and nonchalance.

It's no secret that our band name, Chad's Tree, came from that very band, The Moodists. Gifted to us by simply juggling their first two single titles and, let's face it, anything was better than Orange Ponds.

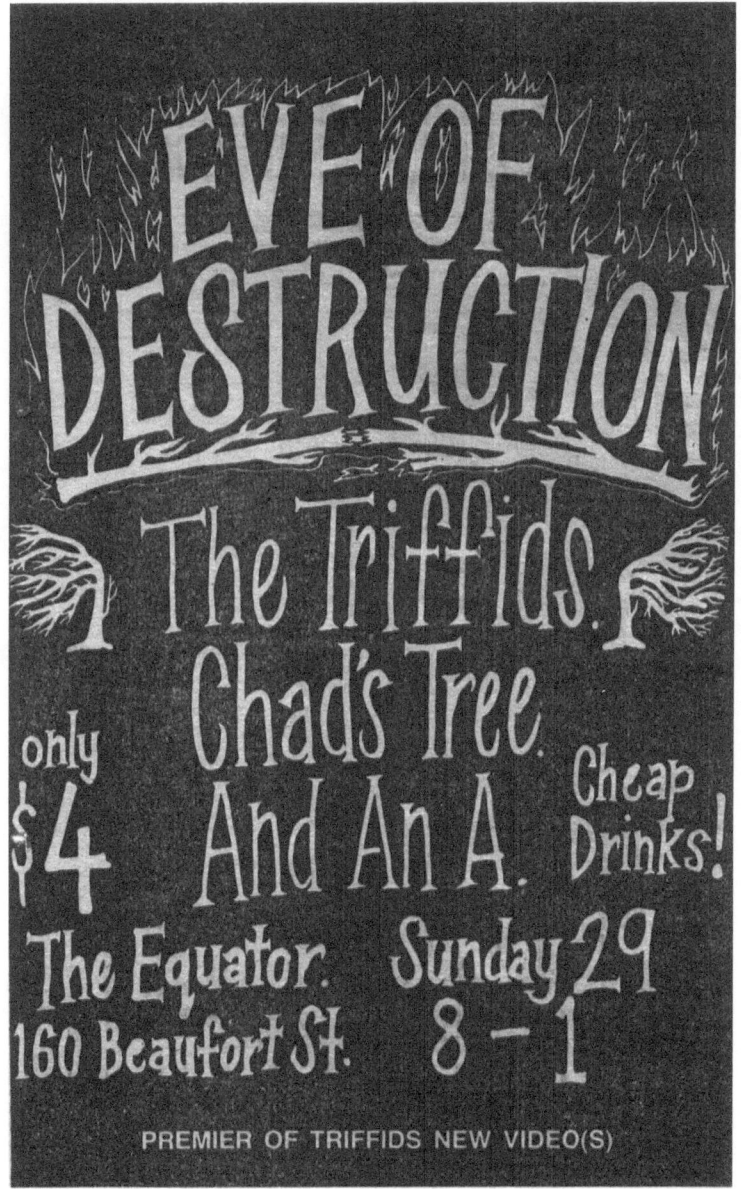

The Aurora Nightclub

Our friend Julianna had insisted a group of us head off to a nightspot she'd recently discovered on William Street. It was open late, there was a band, booze and a stripper. Really? We all followed up the stairs to the Aurora Nightclub wondering what the hell we were in for; we were still youngish and I was hopelessly innocent.

It was part *Number 96*, with a touch of *Twin Peaks* thrown in – I felt lost in another era, half-expecting to have Arnold Feather serve me a Harvey Wallbanger and the Log Lady to step from behind the curtain and sing 'Fever' – but it was 1983; that was never going to happen. There was something charming and something palpably seedy about this place: my first late-night dive.

Sure enough, there was a band, Checkers. A group of middle-aged, overweight, frighteningly adept musicians, playing covers ranging from Roy Orbison, Elvis, Ray Charles, Tony Joe White to The Everly Brothers; I was seriously impressed. They sounded well rehearsed, tight and to my ears bizarrely authentic. For one brief drunken moment, I thought they must have been playing to a backing tape, miming somehow. The audience was at least twice my age, and Roy, the singer, looked a little like a relation on my father's side, but dressed in slightly classier attire. Either someone had slipped something into my drink or I was sitting in the most incredible venue, watching the most phenomenal band this side of the Swan River fronted by a near doppelgänger of my father.

As the band broke between sets, a stripper emerged as promised – part Mary-Anne, part Ginger – was I watching *Telethon* with the cast from *Gilligan's Island*? The music blared, tassels twirled, Julianna whooped and hollered. This was about as wild as it got for my first twenty years on the planet.

Years later, I toured with Lloyd Cole, exchanging the odd tale here and there. He mentioned his first trip to Perth and on one particular night searching for The Triffids who were playing a gig at the Old Melbourne Hotel. He initially stumbled into the front bar, confronted by topless barmaids and barflies, slightly bemused; it left him with an impression that Perth was like a frontier town, part Wild West. Eventually he did find The Triffids and asked if they'd be interested in touring with his band The Commotions throughout Europe. Alas, they'd already been booked to support Public Image in Athens, so things didn't quite pan out. The Triffids ended up being caught in a Greek riot as The Commotions weaved their way through Europe, each with their own story.

The Birthday Party and Jonathan Richman

I had a pretty good idea of what to expect, but I wasn't quite prepared for the relentless assault, the volume or the physical nature of The Birthday Party's first gig in Perth. They had just released *The Bad Seed* EP and were touring WA for the first time.

Nick Cave stalked the long stage of the Red Parrot, contorting his thin, lanky body, doubling over, hooping the microphone lead metres into the air, whiplashing the cord and creating a massive inverted horseshoe. His hair stood tall, splintered, a flaming black sun. He was hassling the stand-in drummer, Des Hefner: gesturing, physically demonstrative, insisting he hit the drum kit harder, demanding to hear more of a crack in the snare.

He appeared intimidating, aggressive, pissed off. Roland S. Howard stared up at the ceiling; I could see the whites of his eyes, his gaunt features and nimble fingers. His Fender Jaguar screeching, shrieking, sending out long, shattering, distorted, piercing notes. Tracy Pew wore black leather pants, a Stetson hat and a serious moustache. He leant backwards precariously, slumping over to the ground on occasions, thumping out brutal, rudimentary harsh bass. They sounded remarkable, they looked remarkable. I felt like a tiny, obedient rodent looking quietly on, petrified.

Half an hour into the set, out of nowhere, came the awkward, bulky, hulking figure of Ray Brown, singer of The Vegas Payback. He launched out from behind the curtains and across the stage, tackled Cave and slammed him to the hard floor. Show over, the band walked off. I remember seeing Brian Hooper too, swaying back there, somewhere in the shadows amongst the mayhem. I'd never heard or seen anything quite like The Birthday Party then, or anything remotely like them since.

I'd heard the debut self-titled album by Jonathan Richman's band, The Modern Lovers, just a handful of times; it was there amongst my brother's record collection. I didn't have any of his solo recordings, but had heard the occasional song.

I wandered into the Red Parrot to the strains of The Jam Tarts, who were opening the night. At this point the sweet harmonies from the girls did little to impress the crowd: a little detached, a tad uninterested, keener to see and hear from Jonathan Richman, no doubt. There was one chap in the audience whose enthusiasm was beyond fandom. He danced, he applauded, he swooned, he hollered out for more, he simply loved The Jam Tarts and single-handedly made up for the flat response the band was receiving. It was Jonathan himself: the one-man audience. It was an unusual, implausibly kind but genuine gesture. After his performance in the audience, he hopped up onto the stage.

He played solo, strummed a nylon string guitar and sang childlike songs for grown-up and half-grown-up people. He was more charming than the ice-cream man and cuter than the little dinosaur he sang about, as he crawled away from the microphone stand, pleading for the little dinosaur not to leave.

He reminisced about summer feelings lost and long gone. Powerful in the most gentle of ways: moving, clever, simple, happy-sad.

So many smiling faces in a usually stiff crowd.

Coo's place, Mt Lawley, 1982.
Mark Beyer, Mark and Rob.

Morrissey Road Party

Twenty-four Morrissey Road was nestled in the yet-to-be-hip pocket of Erskineville. It was a grand, old, stand-alone white terrace house with a little dilapidated front balcony. It had seen better days and our landlord, Mr Kite, was a gracious man who let us run the place as if it were our own. I barely remember an inspection and, let's face it, he was always going to pull it down at some stage, it was only a matter of time.

We had a sort of spare room and a large landing. Bands from interstate or friends passing through who didn't mind forgoing a bit of their privacy could lob on a mattress. We were comrades with fellow musical travellers, The Triffids, White Cross, Tall Tales and True, and Rabbit's Wedding, and every so often there was a visitor making themselves comfortable in our humble abode, finding space somewhere.

We also had many a gathering fuelled by booze and whatever else was around. We were young, a little impetuous and quite social beings. I remember a casual barbeque in the backyard for the launch of Chad's Tree's debut album *Buckle in the Rail* with supportive friends and musician pals drinking

till the cows came home. There were impromptu gatherings when The Triffids arrived back from Europe and on those occasions the beers flowed freely. I remember listening to David McComb reading the poetry of William Blake on our couch with his artist friend Bill; they were arm in arm, a little inebriated, Bill wearing a makeshift cape and impressive, self-drawn Vegemite sideburns.

Then there was the big one: the infamous all-nighter when our male friends dressed as women, and the women dressed as men. Cross-dressing? Hmm. Well, it was hardly *Les Girls*. Whose idea was that? Umm. Friends came from far and wide of our inner-city sanctum, donning frilly dresses and tops, make-up and drawn-on moustaches. What boundaries were we crossing here? Taste was certainly one of them. What would Lou Reed or David Bowie have made of this ... not that they came into the equation.

My friend Freya found a long black number for me to squeeze into and she applied a wad of make-up, found a long black wig and gave me pigtails. I looked like a cross between a Mexican Spice Girl and Boy George's long-lost Lithuanian cousin.

The Sisters of Perpetual Indulgence came along too (men dressed as nuns) so the news must've got out. Let's just say it was a colourful gathering and went late, late, late into the night. The house was brimming. I barely remember a thing, to be honest, except my poor friend, Freya, having to unzip me and plonk me onto my bed upstairs at some ungodly hour. At this point I was living in the bedroom up the top and at the back of the house, with an incredibly narrow and steep staircase running along the wall – the only way to access my room. The lounge room was downstairs, our home's epicentre with the TV, telephone and stereo.

So, the following day, with my poor head feeling like a waterlogged ball I half-awoke wondering why on earth the phone was ringing so loudly and relentlessly by my ear as I stirred from a deep slumber. I opened my eyes and found the phone right there in front of me. Why is the phone here? Why?

'Hello?' said the voice of my brother on the end of the line. 'Just checking in. How was the party?'

As my neurons clicked into gear, I looked around and realised I wasn't actually in my own room at all. In fact, I was in the lounge room and I was lying on a beanbag, completely naked. I could feel the dry make-up caked all over my face. Why was I completely naked on a beanbag in the lounge room? Jesus F. Christ, how did this happen?! Not good, just a tad embarrassing. Nude; terrific. I'll never live this one down.

The house was slowly waking – yep, it was only around 2pm – and one of my housemates, Kenny, was wandering up the stairs, freshly showered, sporting a wry grin.

'Morning, Rob.'

The Moodists

There was a time when my 12" of The Moodists' single 'Runaway' was on high rotation at Morrissey Road. It was thrown on the turntable late at night after several drinks and played pretty loud. The vinyl was by now a little scratched and the needle would occasionally skip.

Chris Walsh's solid gold bass line and the crack of Clare Moore's snare set down a sturdy path for Dave Graney's snarling croon and Steve Miller's and Mick Turner's fine, splintered guitars.

It was like a sonic sock to the jaw, a knockout punch. As if Iggy's crawling, lonesome wolf howl from The Stooges' slow grind 'Dirt' had been tied up in a sack and stolen, somehow reshaped.

It was recorded in London with Victor Van Vugt and released on the Red Flame Label. The cover art features a photograph of the band by Bleddyn Butcher. They look a little aloof, a little wise-cracking, an enigmatic bunch.

One of a handful of Australian bands that left the country in the early 1980s in search of something more, hanging out, recording, touring the UK and Europe, along with The Triffids, The Go-Betweens, The Laughing Clowns and The Birthday Party. All awe-inspiring, idiosyncratic bands: gifted, unique. Creating sounds yet to be heard elsewhere on the planet.

I admire that: leaving, finding a new home, and starting again in a different country. It's romantic, brave, a gamble and a challenge: out of your comfort zone, not knowing what will eventuate; an icy plunge.

My partner Peter did that, left all he knew, his family and friends, and started afresh in London. My brother the same: landed in Madrid knowing only one person and nothing of the language and little of the culture, made friends, found a job and set up a new life in España.

Phil Kakulas

I'd seen Phil Kakulas's new band The Wanderlust Trio upstairs in a long-gone café somewhere on Hay Street, Perth, with my brother, and then again some months later downstairs at the Wizbah. By the second show – and I'm guessing in between times – they'd turned from their Velvet Underground leanings into an experimental, free-form jazz monster. Phil's girlfriend, Sally, was playing drums: belting her kit with a kind of random precision, while some bearded guy was blowing into a PVC pipe. Gone was Dave Bakler and his beautiful black, semi-acoustic, glistening Guild. What happened? Not entirely my cup of tea, but interesting enough.

I remember Sally's and Phil's faces in amongst the crowd when we supported John Cale (possibly wondering how the hell Chad's Tree had landed such a prestigious support) and again, sometime down the track, I noticed Phil's winter-clad shape drifting along the streets of Fremantle.

I went to see another of the Wanderlust's performances at the Fremantle Arts Centre about this time and as they performed, someone slowly unwrapped long sheets of white paper between the scaffolding surrounding them, so they emerged from beneath a vast mesh of white tissue.

Phil and Sally were invited to a slide night at the McCombs' house, The Cliffe, where John McComb was showing some pics from his recent trip to Papua New Guinea. I too went along, with my friend and housemate Julian Miller, a man with a virtually encyclopaedic knowledge of music and, singer with pop meisters Picnic Time. Everyone was affable enough; we all got on well as we watched and listened as John explained the slides, showing us the dense forests, stunning scenery and humble dwellings.

But it wasn't until The Bottomless Schooners of Old toured WA that I got to know Phil a little better. By this time, still in Perth, he was playing double bass in a band with Mexican opera singer and tango queen Rita Menendez. On occasion they were accompanied by an extraordinary virtuoso piano accordionist, Ross Bolleter (an early member of The Blackeyed Susans).

Dave had asked Phil to play percussion and stand-up snare for The Schooners for a handful of WA gigs. This little monstrous holiday band for some of The Triffids, consisting of Dave McComb, 'Evil' Graham Lee, Martyn P. Casey and me, playing an array of covers ranging from Big Star, Prince, Cold Chisel, and Springsteen to Hot Chocolate, Sam Cook, The Rolling Stones and Bob Dylan with a Triffids song or two thrown in for good measure. I had the opportunity to sing a lot of songs for the first time, and in front of healthy crowds. We were ballad animals, purveyors of fine pain: the precursor to The Blackeyed Susans.

The Blackeyed Susans (first line-up, 1989).
Phil Kakulas, Ross Bolletter, Alsy MacDonald, Rob, David McComb (foreground).

The Marrickville Postman

I don't recognise Marrickville these days. It's moved on, and I moved out half a lifetime ago. It's been close to thirty years since I donned the uniform and delivered mail around that sprawling, leafy, inner-west Sydney suburb for Australia Post.

For a time I left my social and musical life behind and became a virtual walking pork chop to all breeds of dog, from Alsatian to Pomeranian. Honestly, fluffy pooches with ribbons in their hair took great delight in attempting to take a bite out of my butt. I love dogs, but back then I was just seen by them as a collection of walking bones, possibly like those grilled ribs on the top of Fred Flintstone's car.

My colleagues at Australia Post were pretty old school. The boss, Billy, was good natured and a bit of a laugh, easygoing and affable. There was one young lass who worked there, poor Jacqui: the vegetarian from New Zealand. Vegetarians made no sense whatsoever to those blokes, who generally enjoyed horseracing, downing a schooner and wolfing a parma at the local pub after work. I'm not sure why but one of the old guys wanted to show Jacqui a men's magazine he'd found in the mailroom early one morning – best not think about that moment.

The rumours were that one of our fellow posties had won Lotto and simply came to work for something to do. Really? That's the best he could come up with. One afternoon I bumped into him snacking on fish and chips quietly by himself on a lonely stretch of beach near Bronte. Weird, guess money can't buy friends, or maybe the fish and chips were too good to share. I don't think he even recognised me that day.

There was another young bloke there who played rugby and drank a lot. He was a big unit from Casino, Queensland, who took great joy in boasting about his wayward antics to anyone who cared to listen. His proudest moment in the big smoke was walking into a local Vietnamese restaurant one Friday night after drinking a bladder-full of beer and proceeding to racially vilify the staff and urinate on the floor. Vile.

My social life became limited and gigs were weekend-only affairs. I could barely stay awake past 10pm. Sorting mail into pigeon holes, stuffing it into a satchel, walking for miles and slotting it into letterboxes was taking its toll. I'm pretty sure the highlight of my weekend had somehow become watching *Hey, Hey, It's Saturday*. I'd now be waking up early in the morning whilst my housemates were coming home from late-night parties and band excursions. My body clock went awry and I felt like all the opportunities for more youthful fun and shenanigans were suddenly drying up. So I simply quit, called it a day and moved into a job with more socially acceptable working hours. Funnily enough, I'd probably appreciate postal hours more these days, though a 5am rise mid-winter could still prove to be a harsh, unwelcome challenge.

I've been back to Marrickville quite a bit in recent times, and nowadays there seems to be a venue around every corner – the Newsagency, Lazy Bones, the Red Rattler, Camelot,

Gasoline Pony. It looks like my old post office has turned into a burgeoning café and all those pooches loitering about wouldn't harm a baby.

Sydney, 1987.
The Bottomless Schooners of Old, Rob, David McComb, 'Evil" Graham Lee and Martyn P. Casey.

The Velvet Underground and Nico

The banana album, otherwise known as *The Velvet Underground & Nico*, is possibly the most played record in my humble vinyl collection. Over time someone has made a very poor attempt to peel off my banana sticker, so it looks a little sad and worn, a bit pink, and a bit rude. It's true what Brian Eno said: it may have only sold several thousand copies but everyone who bought a copy went on to form a band.

Chad's Tree supported John Cale at the Old Melbourne Hotel in Perth on 24 August 1983, a mere six months into our existence. I know the exact date because I made a list of our first six months of shows in the back of a photo album/scrapbook.

My brother and I saw Lou Reed at the Perth Concert Hall in early 1985 as part of the *New Sensations* tour, with innovative guitarist Robert Wolfe Quine (formerly of Richard Hell & The Voidoids) in his touring band. But, for some reason, I never thought I'd see Nico, let alone be there in the same room or be playing in the support band slot.

By 1986 Chad's Tree had relocated to Sydney and we were invited to open for Nico at the Prince of Wales Hotel in St Kilda. This was simply incredible. We'd drive down the Hume Highway, play a show of our own, support Nico for one night and then head back up to Sydney.

The stage was alight with candles and her voice was as beautifully fragile and as haunting as I'd hoped. Such a striking-looking person: her hair auburn with a grey streak or two - no longer the blonde Velvets femme fatale – high cheekbones, a gentle, lilting voice and enchanting German

Chad's Tree, circa 1988 Sydney.
Sue Grigg, Mark Snarski, James Hurst, Rob.

accent. I simply should never talk to anyone I admire, the rubbish that escapes from my mouth. I was backstage and Nico wandered up to me, happy to make herself known. 'You still have such a beautiful voice,' I said. Really, just stop ... is that all my brain could think of for my mouth to blurt out.

Many years before all of this, Nico was romantically linked to Jackson Browne. She recorded an incredible song of his filled with loss and regret called 'These Days' which appears on her debut album *Chelsea Girls*. Browne was a young, precocious writer, apparently having written the song in his teens.

I opened the day's proceedings at *A Day on the Green* at Rochford Winery, when Browne toured Australia in 2003. The highlight for me was being side of stage hearing him sing this humble, poignant song. Incredible how it retained its potency.

It didn't take long for me to become distracted, drawn to my memory of Nico and her achingly beautiful, lonesome, sombre voice.

Paul Kelly

I'd always liked Melbourne. Whenever I came south from Sydney, it appeared more welcoming. It also made more sense to me. There was a grid – a river that divided the St Kilda and Fitzroy music scenes – plus here was the MCG: the home of Australian Rules Football and cricket. The light wasn't as harsh, there was a permanent gloomy haze, the Yarra River was murky and brown, the city grey. It retained a sense of history, you could see it in these buildings – Federation architecture, terrace houses – and there were trams. What's not to love?

I remember visiting in 1985 and I swear that every household I visited was listening to Paul Kelly's album *Post*. The album followed me everywhere or I followed it, extraordinary. Nigel in Carlton, Simone and Jane in Collingwood, Ash and Pete in Elwood. Did I see Paul Kelly and Hunters & Collectors at the Venue in St Kilda with Harem Scarem and Chris Wilson around this time or did I just dream it?

I'd been to the Hopetoun Hotel in Sydney with David McComb earlier in the year to hear Paul Kelly and his band. His guitarist, Steve Connolly, had a beautiful touch and tone and played stunning interweaving melodies and sang the sweetest harmonies. Dave was keen on a song called 'Clean This House'.

After they'd finished their set, Paul Kelly drifted off into the night with Grant McLennan, and Dave and I drifted back to Erskineville.

Years later Paul Kelly wrote 'Summer Leaves', a song for me to sing with The Blackeyed Susans. It appears as a bonus track on the single 'This One Eats Souls' as well as the compilation *Hard Liquor, Soft Music*.

The first time The Blackeyed Susans were invited to tour with Paul Kelly coincided with a Cricket World Cup and a Test Series around Australia. We found ourselves sharing planes with the giants of the cricket-sphere, sometimes seated behind icons of the game. They went about reading their sporting stories in the back pages of the newspapers and we tuned in as they complained about Australian sports journalism.

We arrived in Sydney on the first leg of the tour, prepared for what promised to be big shows. We were going to most capitals and finishing in Perth. The band was waiting at the luggage collection for what seemed an over-long time and our gear simply didn't show up. Nothing. We complained, others complained, they searched... still nothing, zilch. Perplexed by all this, we were then told to call the airline in several hours(!) and hopefully by then they would have located our missing items and sorted through this mess. Consequently, we had to ask Paul and his band if it was possible to share their backline until our gear emerged from the airline's vortex.

So, at sound check at the Metro we fumbled our way through, using what musical gear of theirs we could. Sound check over, I finally managed to speak with someone at the airport who was relieved to pass on the good news that our gear had finally been located and was on its way to the venue. It had somehow been stored with the Sri Lankan side's cricket equipment and was being brought promptly to the Metro in a taxi. I waited on George Street for the promised vehicle, and, sure enough, within half an hour of the call, all our gear arrived intact, along with a pole vault.

The following day we flew off to Adelaide and again we were on the same flight as the Australian cricket side. Some faces were missing. I remember waiting for our gear to arrive at the luggage belt when David Boon appeared from nowhere. I asked for his autograph; sadly he would announce his retirement from international cricket later that day. I still have the ragged green piece of scrap paper –alongside his signature are the autographs of Ian Healy and Mark Waugh, champions of the sport.

As for the music: the tour went well. I was drinking far too much and I remember telling Paul somewhere along the way that we were happy just being their support act, forever, that'd do us just fine. I also remember thinking on one particular night, in a boozy haze, that it would be interesting to stage dive into the sea of people crowding the front at the Fremantle Arts Centre. Thankfully, that didn't happen. Why anyone would do that whilst sharing a Hank Williams song with Paul Kelly is beyond me but at the time it seemed a reasonable thing to contemplate.

Years later I again supported PK nationally with Dan Luscombe and David Creese after the release of *There Is Nothing Here That Belongs to You*, we played all manner of venues including a town hall in Kalgoorlie and the Bunbury Entertainment Centre.

One summer, I managed to write a Christmas song whilst reading Paul's extensive autobiography, inspired by his dry and direct style. Sitting by a pool in Bali, reading, writing, conjuring. I came up with the wintery tune 'Christmas Card from a Drunken Sailor'.

The Blackeyed Susans Sing, Sing Studios, Richmond 1996.
Kiernan Box, Rob, Dan Luscombe, Phil Kakulas, Mark Dawson.

Rob and Dan.

Casino Lights

My father liked to gamble. I have childhood memories of waiting in the car outside the Gosnells TAB with my brother for what seemed like an eternity, with just the car's AM radio for entertainment. We were often on our way to or from Fremantle Oval with our dad on a Saturday afternoon to watch South Fremantle, the mighty Bulldogs.

My folks had also owned a couple of racehorses – Krakus had won a country race and the finishing post photograph sat pride of place on the centre of the mantelpiece for a time.

Dad was mainly a weekend punter, though I do vaguely remember him setting up a phone account. Hmm. My parents worked extremely hard – nonstop – and they had a pretty sedentary social life. When the casino opened in that swampland on the outskirts of Perth, it was as if spring had sprung; there seemed to be a clarion call at all hours of the day and night, and my folks were drawn to those glistening casino lights. My mother knew when to leave, when to walk away … but not my pa. He would push his luck, always gambled on, and on those occasions he was harshly punished.

I'd been living in Sydney for a time, playing with Chad's Tree, but decided to embark on more singing and less guitar noodling, so I moved back to Perth. I needed a casual job as I'd enrolled at university with grand plans to do some further study. I applied for a job as a croupier/blackjack dealer, as the allure of the green felt had kind of got to me too after visiting the casino with my folks several times on my return. I worked night shifts mainly, which would end around 2-3am. Consequently, I'd nod off during my lectures: sleep-deprived, maybe that's why I never understood semiotics. Still, dealing cards was thoroughly engaging, well paid and enjoyable. I saw some pretty outrageous behaviour from the late-night high rollers and frequently the same faces would be there at the start and again at the end of my shift.

I was naïve, I never viewed gambling as a social scourge or an addiction. I saw it as light entertainment for those chasing that elusive rush and the golden dollar.

'Don't split fives, always double against a six, stay sober, leave when you're in front. If you've lost your first wad of cash, call it quits.' These formulated fundamentals ran through my head when I played and now as I dealt out cards to both the gullible and professional gamblers.

I was invited to a poker night held by some of the more experienced staff: a boozy, long night where I didn't win a single hand. I was fleeced, lost all my marbles, lucky to leave with the shirt on my back, totally smashed. Lesson learnt.

I lasted at the casino near on two years before heading off to Europe and the US to spend all my hard-earned savings, see a bit of the world and do a little recording. Subsequently I never returned to that Swan River oasis.

Years later, one Saturday morning, I walked into the family home to find my father and brother sitting either end of the dining table, hunched over, gargoyle-like, studying their own form guides and tuned in to the racing channel, genetic bookends. My poor ma was, of course, busy preparing food in the kitchen.

For me the thrill had dissipated. I developed the philosophy that gambling was actually about losing and dealing with those unhappy consequences, but I know and I've seen that when you're on a roll it's incredibly difficult to resist the pull.

Ocean of You

It was a substantial drive to Tuart Hill from Kelmscott, some 38 kilometres, in fact. I wasn't so familiar with Perth's northern suburbs and I'd never been to Channel 7. I drove there on autopilot, with a trusty road directory, delirious and nervy, having had little sleep the night before, as this early morning television appearance was playing havoc with my mind. I'd been on TV before. In Chad's Tree music videos, as an extra in a couple of Australian dramas (including a mini-series with Nicole Kidman), and then once singing backing vocals on Clive Robertson's late show in Sydney with The Triffids. Never singing solo and never on *Good Morning Perth*.

The show was hosted by the effervescent Jenny Clemesha, and the early morning start meant I had a quick run-through before going live to air. I was performing 'Ocean of You', a song penned by David McComb: the first he'd written specifically for me to sing. A beautiful tango-esque ballad, part drowning, part treading water in a sea of love and its myriad complications.

I wore my best op-shop jacket and slicked back my hair. I sat there on a stool under the heat of the lights as the cameramen got their angles and pieced together how it might look, then my quick run-through. The producer said I'd be on after the ad and next segment, and away I went. It's all a complete blur, of course, but I do remember another young guest applauding alongside her mother. I suppose we singers need that little reward, the instant gratification. It's not like our sound is produced by a stringed instrument, you don't simply pick it up, pluck away and plonk it back in its case. It emanates from our body, chest, throat and head. The voice - troublesome, temperamental, demanding – hence our neediness, I suspect.

Jenny Clemesha kindly mentioned a Blackeyed Susans show that was coming up at the Old Melbourne Hotel, and thanked me for coming on the show. I packed my guitar into its case and headed out to the car park. It was all over by 9am. I chucked the guitar in the boot and navigated the roads straight back home to Kelmscott with an enormous sense of relief. Nothing awful happened; I'd managed to remember the chords and the entire lyrics without a hiccup, thankfully.

My father was waiting at the front door, looking pretty chuffed. He'd sat there at home in the lounge room, surrounded by a sea of red shag pile, and watched his youngest son on the box, singing and strumming away. He said I'd looked like Lou Diamond Phillips and it sounded so crisp and clear, not like those bloody awful venues he'd popped into. In fact, he was so impressed he'd rung Channel 7 over a dozen times, disguising his voice on each occasion, saying how sensational that young singer was and insisting they invite him back on the show.

Pig and Salmon

There was a pig's head in the sink, blood forming a deep red pool that swirled slowly down the drain of the gleaming silver stainless steel. I happened to mention this casually to my schoolmates, Graham and Chris, who didn't quite believe me, but, sure enough, as they wandered out through the kitchen, there it was staring up at them. They were horrified at the sight, managing a nervous laugh between them as they moved quickly out the door.

Dad had raised three pigs and named them after his two sons and our friend Ewen; I'm not sure which one this was.

Graham (Poundy) and Chris were my best friends at school. On the weekends in our teens we either played in the same losing football or cricket side or rode about the surrounding bushland on our motorbikes. They'd occasionally hang out at our place to watch TV and have a bite to eat. Poundy had only recently recovered from being pursued and traumatised by our villainous giant of a turkey, Ivan the Terrible. Now there was a pig's head in the sink: welcome to the world of Snarski.

Another of my schoolfriends, Louie, reminded me of a time he was sitting in the back of our family car, concerned he may have been bitten by a spider. For some reason we weren't overly concerned; instead we found it amusing, we laughed.

Years later, The Blackeyed Susans' second Perth line-up featured the remarkable, unparalleled talent that is Kim Salmon. Kim sang and played guitar in a particular visceral way that somehow managed to intrigue our numerous geese. The flock gathered by the large bedroom window where we rehearsed, looking in directly at Kim whenever he came to the microphone. They sat still, focused on him just beyond the large glass window pane. With the song reaching its climax, our grey feathered friends suddenly raised themselves onto their orange webbed feet. They all ran full-tilt in a long line towards the neighbouring fence, back and forth, repeatedly, wings and necks outstretched, honking vehemently, convincing us all that they approved. This was their form of adulation, human worship.

The Blackeyed Susans (second line-up, 1990), Perth.
Adrian Wood, Kim Salmon, Alsy MacDonald, Martyn P. Casey, Rob.

Sing the Song

Dave McComb was forever encouraging me to put myself in the spotlight, to get out there and sing. At times random, unexpected moments. There were also instances where he was frustrated, drained by my lack of confidence, my anxiety, insecurities and, frankly, my inability to deliver a lyric, culminating in some delicate and brutal home truths in the studio.

'SING THE SONG!'

We were at a Bob Dylan tribute night at The Piccadilly Hotel in the backstreets of Kings Cross one night: watching, listening, having a quiet drink. Halfway through the night, Dave thought it would be a good idea for me to get up there and sing a Dylan tune. *What? How?* I wondered. No guitar, unannounced.

'Just borrow something, I'll ask,' coaxing me to do it, persisting. Before too long I was standing on the stage singing 'Spanish Is the Loving Tongue' to a very still and attentive gathering. It was certainly not in my character to do something that spontaneous with zero time to think about it;

I'm certainly not the wildest or freest of individuals. If it were left up to me, maybe I wouldn't have sung much at all apart from warbling away in my bedroom or the family car.

I gathered my composure and my fingers found their way around the loaned guitar as the MC for the night introduced me. You could hear a pin drop in the audience and the song was well received. Dave could pick these moments. I sang Prince's 'The Cross' with The Triffids when they were passing through Sydney in a similar spontaneous moment and around the same time he insisted I hop on board to sing backing vocals on 'Trick of the Light' when they performed under the green television studio glow on a late-night show with Clive Robertson. They had returned home from London having completed their most sonically ambitious album to date, *Calenture*, with an extensive national tour in place.

Dave was a generous being, one who wanted his friends to share this musical ride of his. His own confidence carrying you, your own insecurities impeding, counteracting his creative and supportive efforts.

I was in London for a time when he, Kenny Davis Jnr and I ended up recording an album's worth of songs at Island Studios.

Dave had been in contact with my brother in Spain, who would contribute songs; Phil too. The plan was to record some of Dave, Mark and Phil's new songs plus a selection of covers we'd reinterpret. It would be a late-night record: ballads, lonesome songs. My role was simply to sing and to play as little guitar as possible. Kenny and Dave would work on the arrangements. So we rehearsed the songs in Bleddyn and Jude's lounge room in Whitechapel, and in Dave and Jo's in Ladbroke Grove for several days before heading into Island Studios in Chiswick to whittle away. Four of those songs ended up on The Blackeyed Susans' vinyl EP *Depends What*

You Mean by Love the rest sit on a DAT tape, in a box, in a cupboard ...somewhere.

There was a significant 'sing the song' moment at Island as I was grappling with the delivery of a particular lyric, the spine of the song. I can only imagine how draining this recording would have been from Dave's and Kenny's viewpoints. For me the London recordings mostly bolstered my confidence but to a certain extent it was crushing – a mature-age apprenticeship with a harsh lesson in self-realisation. Maybe I could just sing a tune but not necessarily deliver a song.

Whitechapel rehearsal, 1990.
David McComb, Rob and Kenny Davis Junior.

First Song

In my mid-teens I wrote a song based on my brother's first long-term relationship with his high-school girlfriend at the time, Penny. I simply lifted the title of The Beatles' song 'The Ballad of John and Yoko' and switched it rather conveniently to 'The Ballad of Penny and Mark'. I was never sued by Apple. Thankfully no-one ever heard it; I can't remember the lyrics, or the tune for that matter ... shame.

I'd started collaborating with Phil Kakulas on songs for *Mouth To Mouth*. At this point I had very few co-writing credits with The Blackeyed Susans, but Phil and I had been busy working on this new batch and I was contributing to the music in bigger chunks – melodies, chord progressions and simple arrangement ideas. It was a very creative and productive period for me. Phil and I were sharing a house in East Brunswick with The Blackeyed Susans' manager, Linda Gebar, at the time. We'd all moved from a spacious abode in North Fitzroy to what seemed like friggin' miles north, to the outskirts of Melbourne's civilisation: East Brunswick. I'd only ever passed this way heading to the airport. This was a smaller, homelier place owned by Tom Morton, the brother of our friend Rosy. Rosy owned a bookshop in town, played the drums and was married to my pal Gordy, who played bass in The Coral Snakes.

Phil and I had been working on songs together ever since the band started to unravel. Essentially Dave McComb was now pursuing his solo career, focusing on his debut release *Love of Will*. Graham Lee and Warren Ellis were now going off overseas with Dave as part of his band The Red Ponies. It looked very much like the Melbourne Susans' personnel were drifting off and the band had begun to rapidly dissolve. We were left to work out if there were songs within us to keep the flame burning, and if it was worth persevering with two remaining fragments of what perhaps could still be The Susans.

We'd recently found Kiernan Box, whilst on an ill-fitting regional comedy tour. We played in trio mode with Mark C. Halstead on vocals and mandolin, closing the night and bringing everyone tumbling back down to earth after an onslaught of young enthusiastic comedians. Comedy and The Blackeyed Susans Trio ... who would have thunk it.

KB was playing piano interludes for a troupe called The Black Cabs, tinkling away, skipping from Lou Reed to Tom Waits or a jazz piece, songs of his choice. One night he dropped in the riff to the Susans' song 'A Curse on You' and to this point we still hadn't spoken to one another. Kiernan's a unique piano player and an interesting character. During rehearsals he'll somehow read *War and Peace* or *Tintin* (in Indonesian) whilst wandering fingers flow over the ivories, not losing the time or the plot. What's KB building in there, we sometimes wonder.

Phil and I had been working on these new songs for a while now. He had set up his Tascam four-track recorder in his room. Firstly, he'd program a rudimentary drum track, then add his bass. I'd add rhythm guitar and we'd overdub musical ideas as the lightbulb moments occurred. Phil at the time was prolific, lyric-writing brimming. I recall him saying at one stage that it was lucky for me he was still around, otherwise I'd just be singing 'blah, blah, blah'.

I hadn't written a set of lyrics worthy of recording with the BES and I was wondering if I was even capable of producing something that could stand alongside Phil or Dave, or anyone for that matter. Those two had been writing songs since their teens, numerous co-writes in the very early, and then again in the very late, days of The Triffids. I considered myself lucky enough just to be the singer. Earlier in Chad's Tree with my brother Mark, I'd contributed melodic lines in arrangements, but songs themselves, and lyrics, were seemingly out of my grasp. I appeared to always be standing there in the shadows.

One night after a productive bout of demo-ing I wandered off to my room. It took some time to drift off and when I did, I floated into a light, simple dream in which Juliet from The Lighthouse Keepers was lingering by the banks of a river singing a single line over and over. I was becoming conscious of this in my sleep and fought to pull myself out of my slumber. I reached across and switched on my bedside lamp and found my humble recording device. My guitar was leaning against the wall, at arm's length, so I lay on the bed singing the few words Juliet had sung, found the chords that fitted around the melody and softly warbled away. I lay there for a couple of hours, guitar on belly, half-asleep, half-awake, continuing to formulate verses and a chorus to a jagged, staccato rhythm. Being in this sleep-like state seemed to help drive the writing process: less self-conscious, less dismissive, it seemed to flow. I jotted down the fragmented ideas of the lyric on loose sheets of A4 paper, scribbled away, crossing lines out here and there. It was taking on a voyeuristic, obsessive shape, themes The

Blackeyed Susans could easily dabble with. I was nearly there; it appeared almost complete, and then again sleep pulled me under. No-one visited me in my dreams this time and I awoke several hours later with my guitar by my side and the lyric sheets strewn on the bed around me.

I remember sitting at the red laminex kitchen table the following morning and playing 'I Need You' to Phil after breakfast. He was curious that I could dream a song, eager and quietly encouraging. He was also able to recognise that the song was lacking a vital element, in need of a slight twist. He came up with a lyrical idea to bring the song to a more foreboding climax. It was done.

Perceptive, he can assist with songs when you've lost motivation or clarity. Step into your shoes for that brief moment and make a song worthy.

When it was time to demo in the following days, I remember suggesting blowing into half-filled, musically tuned beer stubbies to provide a deepish whistle: a dreamy sound, adrift, like a ship lost at sea.

Jim and Warren

I was standing on the stage amongst puddles of water. Rain had escaped the inadequate covering, dripped and formed little lakes around the band. Surely this couldn't be good: historically electricity and water have never been the greatest of companions.

Moomba long weekend and Chad's Tree were one of several bands playing out here on this soggy structure. I'd strapped on my Telecaster, plugged it into my Music Man and avoided stepping too close to any of the damp spots. There weren't many folk around, given the inclement weather, grey skies, chilly winds. I certainly knew where I'd rather be.

The Feral Dinosaurs were playing too: a country trio with Conway Savage on piano, Jim White on drums and a very tall chap called Jim Shugg playing guitar. I vaguely remember those guys being under this makeshift tent, watching us from out there with the handful of people that had braved the Melbourne skies.

I saw The Feral Dinosaurs play again sometime after, possibly in Prahran upstairs, where they packed out a joint called IDs (before it became the Continental). Their reference points were Jerry Lee Lewis and Hank Williams, though Jim White drummed more like a jazz drummer, closer to Jeffrey Wegner in style than a country player ... I liked them a lot.

Sometime down the track Chad's Tree passed through Melbourne again and I stayed at Jim's, in a share house, when he was playing drums in a band called Fungus Brains with Mick Turner. We had a few beers and listened to George Jones. I caught him next at the Punter's Club, Fitzroy, in a group called Busload of Faith. Megan Bawden, their singer, was smart and lean, more Patti Smith than Lou Reed (as the band name suggested). There was a primal, dark-eyed chap with massive sideburns that would put a pirate to shame playing a fiercely charged violin: 'twas Warren Ellis.

It was 1992. The Blackeyed Susans had relocated to Melbourne and we were in search of musicians after the previous year in Sydney where, we'd poached members of The Cruel Sea, The Jackson Code and Pressed Meat and The Smallgoods to record the four-track EP *Anchor Me* and tour briefly.

After seeing Busload of Faith I asked Jim if he'd be at all interested in playing drums with the Susans and if he knew of anyone who played piano and/or accordion. Jim was quite keen and mentioned Warren may be interested, accordion being his first instrument. So, when Dave finally arrived back from Europe, via Perth, we began rehearsing.

Even then Warren was a take-no-prisoners musician: quick-witted, audacious. I remember getting a lift around St Kilda in his Holden HR with The Sun Ra Arkestra blaring out of his car radio speakers. I couldn't concentrate, let alone negotiate Punt Road traffic. Seemingly, Warren was oblivious to complete chaos.

We were in Adelaide opening for Concrete Blonde at a nightclub called Heaven. After our set, and having consumed his fair share of the drinks rider, Warren decided to explore the main act's band room in search of what they might have that we didn't. He emerged moments later, staggering down the hallway, carrying a massive coffee machine with its long lead trailing behind him, insisting we set it up somewhere in our room.

After a weekend of shows in Sydney, Dave and Warren started singing Bowie songs at the top of their lungs. It was entertaining for us but I'm not sure if the other passengers on the 747 appreciated it quite as much: still, no harm done. We exited the plane and headed off to baggage collection. It's the only time I've ever seen anyone on the actual luggage belt searching for an item: Warren disappeared behind the wall and emerged again on the opposite side. Needless to say, the airport staff weren't overly impressed.

Linda Gebar started managing The Susans sometime after *All Souls Alive* was released. Prior to this 'Handsome' Steve Miller looked after the books, with little to no pay or appreciation. The band too was starting to unravel at this point. Linda had been busy managing Frente! and The Killjoys. She noticed how little work we'd done to promote the CD, so she quickly plotted a tour of the East Coast for a meagre trio of Susans to fulfil. Even then it was painfully difficult to find a third member of this dissipating bunch of minstrels willing to commit. Eventually Warren, Phil and I headed north in my trusty Camira station wagon with a double bass, two amps, acoustic guitar, violin and accordion loaded in the back. The neck of the double bass was precariously placed between the two front seats, just over the gearstick. It was a tad cramped; there were feet on the dashboard and musicians' debris everywhere else, but we fitted. We drove for miles and played to crowds in Sydney, Canberra, Byron Bay, Brisbane and Noosa.

JIM AND WARREN

Somehow in Noosa we were billed as Perth's hottest acid-jazz band and were virtually run out of town. At the Great Northern in Byron Bay they expected us to bring a PA so we adapted, and played semi-unplugged. I wandered through the crowd and serenaded folks sitting at the tables.

I recall Warren's tasteful rendition of 'I've Got a Lovely Bunch Of Coconuts' on his trusty accordion at the Zoo in Brisbane's Fortitude Valley, and at one point in Sydney he disappeared, went completely AWOL. I had a hunch he might just be hanging out with his St Kilda comrades also up from Melbourne on tour. Maurice Frawley and The Working Class Ringos were staying in Kings Cross and there was only one place to look: the Hotel New Hampshire. Sure enough, when Phil and I eventually convinced the concierge to let us into their hotel room late in the morning, we found Warren snoozing on a couch amongst discarded pizza boxes and empty beer cans, alongside overflowing ashtrays.

We helped Warren gather up his belongings and then hit the road. After a quick-fire drive, our dishevelled trio performed somewhere in Canberra University, following a stand-up comedian. At one point the comic reeled off ten numbers, and then sometime later into his routine he asked if anyone in the audience could repeat the numbers. Warren was quick to respond, numbers precisely in their sequence.

I'm not exactly sure how we survived that tour. One whiff of my car was enough to anaesthetise a small marsupial. Luckily for Warren we'd budgeted well and planned to fly him home from the Gold Coast. A quick hug farewell and then Phil and I continued the sapping drive home to Melbourne, with a stop-off halfway in sunny Dubbo to partially recuperate.

The Blackeyed Susans, Melbourne 1993.
Phil Kakulas, Warren Ellis, Jim White, 'Evil' Graham Lee, Rob, David McComb (bottom left).

The Punter's Club

Melbourne, 1995, and *Mouth to Mouth* had been released in Australia on Hi-Gloss/MDS. The Blackeyed Susans were playing to a healthy crowd at the Punter's Club, Brunswick Street, in the heart of Fitzroy. Things had been going well for the band, the personnel had almost settled. Mark Dawson was yet to move down from Queensland to steady the ship so, at this point, old pal Ash Davies from White Cross was thumping the tubs.

A young Dan Luscombe was brimming with exuberance and ideas, Kiernan Box was pounding the keys, part jazz, part Box, and Phil and I were back in electric mode. There was a certain lustful urgency to the new batch of songs, noise and melodrama.

The Dave Last Orchestra (DLO) had opened proceedings on this particular night. Dave Last was quite the frontman; he took his cues from big guns like Elvis and James Brown. There was the occasional knee drop and, if my memory serves me well, even a draped cape ... always a grand entrance and exit. On this occasion Dave was told by the venue there was absolutely no chance he could ride his Harley through the crowd to join his bandmates on stage. Fumes, OH&S, people being run over – they presented a convincing argument, obviously a few safety risks. We all got the impression, however, that Dave was still a little pissed off... even so, DLO put on a fine show.

The Susans' set was in full swing: new songs being well received, the crowd jammed in up close, expectant, and then without warning a young, unassuming chap appeared on the stage and promptly made his way to the microphone. He simply asked everyone to calmly make their way to the exits and evacuate the building. What? At that moment I had no idea this chap, Richard Moffat, was the booker of the venue; we'd never met before and he looked far too young to be running gigs, let alone be in a pub without his parents. He informed us that their bar staff had just received an anonymous phone call. Apparently a bomb had been placed in the building.

Linda Gebar, BES manager, 1994–1996.

Specialist police from the bomb squad would be arriving shortly: he insisted we all leave the premises immediately.

About a third of the crowd dispersed in a mild panic, whilst the rest of us waited anxiously across the street, a little spooked. Gordy, my pal from Belfast, had little time for these types of shenanigans so he and his wife Rosy took the next tram north.

After forty minutes or so, we were given the all clear, the band was able to pick up where it left off, a little shaken, slightly confused and majorly sceptical. Free drinks for all who remained and the Susans kicked on and upped the ante.

Thankfully, no bomb hidden in the back of the pinball machine. A strange, perplexing, mysterious night of music and mayhem.

Babcia

Babcia had been unwell for some time, in fact years before she arrived in Victoria. I fetched her from the airport and escorted her to her new abode, a nursing home in Sorrento. My parents had decided to move from WA after being away from their sons for far too long; I was supposedly more reliable than Mark, who was still at this point living in Sydney. My folks were convinced I was far less likely to take off to parts unknown.

They'd bought a place in Rosebud on the Mornington Peninsula, with the nursing home only a few kilometres away. Dementia had started to affect Babcia's thought processes; she believed she was on holidays in a nice motel and occasionally would ask the staff if there was anything she could do to help. As the years progressed, so did her decline. Communication had always been limited between the two of us; my limited Polish combined with her pidgin English was just enough to get by.

My parents had settled into their new home and we'd visit Babcia on occasion; they were closer and saw her more frequently. Dad had been unwell too, so it was an incredibly stressful time for my hardworking mother, juggling her duties.

I was oblivious to all the anxiety and pressure this must have been causing them, lost in my own stress-free world.

I rang my parents to see how Babcia was faring after some recent health complications. My mother answered the phone and the tone in her voice was sombre.

'How's Babcia?' I asked.

My mother asked me to sit down as the news was not good.

'Why? What's happened?' My thoughts suddenly racing due to my mother's uncharacteristic melancholic tone.

'Babcia died,' Mum said softly.

What? What happened? I didn't think her illness was so serious. How?

'When is the funeral?' I asked.

'We had it today,' she said.

I was stunned, taken aback.

'What? Why didn't you tell me?'

My mother reminded me of how upset I was when my grandfather had passed away. Babcia had suddenly thrown herself on the open coffin at the funeral parlour, grief-stricken, and that image stayed with me for some years. I reminded my mother that I was nine years old at the time; now I was in my thirties and slightly more capable of dealing with death. I seem to remember my father saying he had no regret in not telling me when he was subsequently handed the phone. All I wanted was to have an opportunity to say goodbye, now I was getting upset for all the wrong reasons.

Years later I found out through my cousin that my father hadn't notified his brother in the UK that their mother had passed away, something I still cannot comprehend. Then again, people are prone to some rather odd behaviour when it comes to death and dealing with grief.

Babcia's ashes remained in a tub at my parents' place for several years. She had requested at some point to be buried with my grandfather in Karrakatta Cemetery in WA, which was now implausible. Peter instead suggested that we take her ashes with us on our next planned visit to Perth. Sure enough, Babcia came with us on the plane as carry-on luggage and we made a trip out to Karrakatta on a beautiful, blue-sky Perth day.

We found my grandfather's grave amongst the Polish Catholic section. It had been years since I'd been here and weeds had appeared in little parts around the edges. His bespectacled black and white portrait was looking out from the grey-black headstone. I emptied the contents on top of the slab, and said a few words. Finally they'd been reunited, sort of.

It seemed that within minutes the wind picked up and swirled about, and dark storm clouds suddenly hovered overhead; the weather turned. Now big heavy drops fell from above and we took shelter under those tall ancient pines around the perimeter of the cemetery to save ourselves from being drenched. Maybe in retrospect this wasn't such a good idea, who knows, perhaps their reunion wasn't going so well after all.

Jozefa Snarska ... Babcia.

An Incident in Glebe

I tried heroin once when I was nineteen or twenty, not really thinking of the consequences. A drug mythologised by countless musicians from Lou Reed and David Bowie to Billie Holiday and Keith Richards, and in a song or two. Was that some sort of lame reason to try it? Probably. I was completely naïve and expected complete euphoria, a rush of creativity, but I felt nothing but nauseous and tired; I just wanted to lie down and/or throw up.

I had a gig that night at the Wizbah with Chad's Tree and placed a bucket behind my amp just in case. I was hot and clammy, and felt sick for three entire days, repelled enough to never try it again.

A couple of members of The Susans dabbled for a time; I assumed their experience was completely different to mine. In the early '90's, we were touring and staying at the Rooftop Hotel in Glebe with a couple of gigs booked up in Sydney. A potent batch was being sold on the streets; they were dropping like flies, someone had said.

We were nearly ready to head out to the venue, just waiting on one guy, half the band having headed off earlier. Phil and I knocked on his door, almost ready, just one more thing to do. After stuffing about in the bathroom for a time, Dave came out and sat on the bed, quite chatty but a little anxious and nervy, then mid-sentence, without warning, he slumped over, losing consciousness. Phil and I looked at each other, stunned. It was terrifying: he'd stopped breathing; suddenly he was turning blue as the colour drained from his face. We needed to act quickly. I tried a little CPR without luck and then we rushed to the hotel reception and asked in a panicked state for them to call an ambulance. The guy manning the desk was completely blasé and a little reluctant to do so: not hotel policy or something. 'Would you rather call an ambulance or have a dead person in one of your rooms?' He rang for an ambulance.

It all seemed to happen so quickly. We rifled through Dave's belongings, trying to find the source, and before too long the paramedics turned up and administered some Narcan to reverse the effects of the overdose. Within a minute or so he sat bolt upright with a look of complete confusion and wonder. He was so pale to begin with, and then the colour slowly returned to his face and lips. It took a while for everything to register and for Dave to comprehend what was going on around him; time began to move again. What a relief, thank Christ.

The paramedics left, job done. It was as if the last few moments were simply wiped away and we could head down to the pub to play, which is exactly what we did. We three piled into the hire car, adrenaline coursing through our veins, reeling from the event, and made our way along Parramatta Road.

We walked in. Robert Forster had finished his support slot; he was backstage, dressed in a smart houndstooth jacket, and was slightly disappointed there weren't a few more familiar faces in the audience.

We were now running late, so we quickly explained to our fellow band members what had happened and before too long we were all on stage, playing songs and trying to comprehend the aberration of the night.

Pizza Guy

I don't think you can consider delivering pizzas the most dazzling job, but, for whatever reason, for a period of time there seemed to be a floating line-up of local musicians at a pub I worked at very briefly in East Melbourne: a Coral Snake here, a Killjoy there, and that cool guy Tom from Luxedo. Combine pizza delivery with what is commonly referred to in the hospitality industry as being the 'dish pig', and it was hardly the most glamorous job. There was just a bit too much swagger, bluster and bravado, black clothes and black boots going on in this joint, which seemed incongruous given the menial and grimy tasks we undertook.

I'd actually played in this pub years before with my brother Mark in our band Chad's Tree. What I remember, apart from a very small crowd, was the door girl Anna spilling her drink all over our guest list, and legendary Melbourne music fan and chef extraordinaire Julian Wu leaping up on stage to perform a cracking version of the Triffids classic, 'Butterfly'. The band had given up at this point and simply decided to leave the stage and start up an open-mic night.

Rob, Abbotsford, 2001.

I had no idea there was a red light district in East Melbourne until I had to deliver meals to some of the women who worked around the corner from the pub. I was privy to some interesting conversations on occasion; quite a lot goes on in those dark backstreets.

I remember having a solo gig around this time too, up in North Fitzroy at a venue run by Mikel Simic, aka Mikelangelo, and his family at the Truffula Tree now known as the Pinnacle. After settling in, I noticed there was something scrawled across my face in black texta on one of the posters on the wall. Sure enough, one of my compatriots from the pub had written over my solemn expression 'I'll have a small Hawaiian with mushrooms'.

One night whilst I was driving about delivering pizzas in my beaten-up Camira, my soundtrack was a newly acquired cassette of the majestic instrumental Melbourne trio The Hungry Ghosts, featuring JP Shilo. I was transfixed by one of their songs, 'Nowness'. At some point on Victoria Parade, East Melbourne, I felt compelled to pull over as a set of lyrics literally started to pour out, inspired by this slow, somniferous piece of music. It was an intense stream-of-consciousness experience, as if I was just the body that occupied the thoughts and held the pen. Seriously, I'd never experienced anything like that before, or since. Essentially the lyrics wrote themselves and the pizzas went cold.

It became a song called 'I Can't Find You', this collaboration of sorts with The Hungry Ghosts which I've been lucky enough to sing with them, and release myself, on the album with Dan Luscombe *There Is Nothing Here That Belongs To You*. I'm quietly proud of that song, spooked by that mysterious experience and the inspiration that drifted by in that solitary moment.

Occasionally I still walk past that pub on my way to the MCG. It seems to have become more popular and fashionable, though I never go in. Then I walk past those footy vans, where I once worked too before everything required an official sanction from the AFL.

Father

He was standing chest high in the cold creek water, struggling for hours trying to save one of our milking cows. Tuba had lost her footing and slipped into the deep creek at the bottom of the gully, unable to lift herself out. She was in search of her calf on the opposite side. We held torches and watched Dad battle to keep Tuba's head above the slow-moving water beside the tall grass and white lilies. He was immersed in the creek for hours, well into the night, and there was little he could do; they were both exhausted, the beast traumatised. The tractor and the variety of ropes we'd gathered only prolonged the inevitable. She was bogged down, little chance to save her.

Whilst he was working alone on the orchard spraying the trees, the spray tank's heavy rotating device caught onto and took hold of my father's loose shirt. The motor threw him over onto the hard gravel and snapped his tibia. He managed to drag himself along the hard dirt to the house and phone for an ambulance. To drag himself along the ground over 80 metres, somehow coping with the pain of the break, would have been unbearable. He was in a cast for seven weeks and still managed to drive the tractor around the orchard and go about his usual seasonal chores.

Mum was away visiting us in Sydney when Dad experienced his first heart attack. He had shortness of breath, and chest pains were causing discomfort. Recognising these symptoms, he opted to drive himself to the hospital several kilometres away, his judgement clouded. My grandmother was told to sit in the passenger seat (having never driven before) and my father suggested that if he passed out, she could grab a hold of the steering wheel and guide them the rest of the way. Thankfully he made it. Days later, after a bypass operation, he had a pizza delivered to his ward.

I hadn't been to visit my folks for quite some time. It was a decent drive from Abbotsford to Rosebud and I was becoming slack in my family duties, busy with music and distracted by my social life. Their lounge room looked somehow different: sparser, almost barren. I realised that the bookcases were

Lake Victoria, Koja, Uganda 1945.
Joe and John Snarski.

nearly completely empty. Mark and I had kept some of our books there – Sartre, Dostoyevsky, Camus, Carver, McEwan, Capote, Calvino, Dylan, amongst others - but they'd been moved somewhere. Where? Dad had decided to mulch them for the garden. There wasn't anything worthy of reading in that lot anyway, he explained. Even my mother's biology and science books had gone to tree heaven. He brashly defended his actions: this was completely rational; all that remained on the shelf was an old Oxford Dictionary.

Honey

For several years I lived solo in a small block of aqua-powdery blue-green flats in Abbotsford. Chrysler Lodge, Valiant Street. This regal block was home to a pair of retired nuns, there was a young hipster couple upstairs, a charming lady called Leonie Loveday next door, and me.

The couple upstairs engaged in the loudest sex imaginable. People would literally stop on our quiet street and look up in horror, wondering if anyone was being attacked. Who knows what went on up there. I'd grown so accustomed to it, I just ignored the goings-on, but Lord knows what the nuns thought.

Some new tenants had moved in over the road, students, I think. With them they brought a cat – a meandering, inquisitive, tortoise-shelled, precious fluffy beast – I called her Honey. This delightful fluffball would drop by fairly regularly for a visit and a chat. Meowing away and preening herself, rubbing her face along my legs, generally just hanging out, shooting the breeze. At some point I decided to buy a little cat food and then fed her on the odd occasion. Before too long she started to sleep at the end of my bed. I guess that's not supposed to happen, though, is it? I was caught: hook, line, sinker.

One morning I opened the front gate to be confronted by one of the young students, who launched into a tirade, complaining that her cat had been coming over the road to visit the flats and someone had obviously been feeding her. She pointed over my shoulder, saying Honey was trapped inside and she could see her through the window. Gulp! I turned around slowly and, to my astonishment, Honey wasn't actually in my flat but hanging out with the nun downstairs. I guess she'd fallen for Honey too. Honey was now parading up and down the windowsill, seeking the exit, meowing in mime. We couldn't hear a thing, but she was putting on a convincing act of looking distressed and feeling trapped, fully fed, no doubt.

It wasn't long after that I bought a place with Peter in Westgarth and consequently left my marine-motor-wonder-world. This love affair with Honey was going to be a difficult relationship to break off. I wasn't sure how to leave her; this was going to be tough on both of us.

The night I finally moved out I remember being surrounded by a mix of the old and new things, piled up randomly with little space to arrange furniture. It was happy chaos, but the sight of it was exhausting. My mind wandered. I couldn't help but think of sweet abandoned Honey. Maybe she was waiting for me to come home so she could be fed for the third time, or possibly she was wondering where she might be sleeping at night's fall. She would be feeling anxious, lost, lonesome.

Somehow I convinced Peter that it was a sane enough idea to go over there and just double-check. So we both hopped in the car and drove ten minutes down Hoddle Street, over to Chrysler Lodge. Sure enough, there she was, poor Honey, waiting outside my gate. I picked her up and sneakily popped her into the car. Yes, I'd also managed to convince Peter that she should stay one night in our new place and then I'd graciously return her the next day. Obviously this was nuts. Did I care what the students, nuns or sexually charged neighbours thought? No.

So we drove back to the bedlam of our new abode with Honey meowing and purring all the way. It was my way of saying goodbye, and we simply took her back to her Abbotsford home the following morning.

Farewell, sweet Honey.

Melbourne Cup 2010.
Rob and Peter.

Leonard Cohen

Phil Kakulas persisted: he convinced Mick Newton, one of the organisers of *A Day on the Green*, we would be the perfect support for Leonard Cohen at his forthcoming show in the Yarra Valley. Leonard Cohen had not toured Australia for what seemed like decades. In the meantime he'd lost his fortune, been ripped off by his manager, and found himself on the bones of his arse, so some heavy touring was in order. It's rare when an opportunity to be musical guests for someone of this calibre comes your way. The Blackeyed Susans would open the day's proceedings, with Paul Kelly and nephew Dan, performing in the middle spot. Euphoria.

On the afternoon of the gig, I remember driving along the winding roads of the Dandenongs, past the dense forests of tall, straight eucalypts and massive tree ferns, desperate to get to sound check on time. Finally, out into the vast green countryside of the Yarra Valley, nearing Rochford.

Brilliant day, big blue skies, light winds, picture perfect for an outdoor concert. I arrived at the entry gate and chatted quickly to the security folk, was given directions and loading instructions and then I heard, drifting through on that light breeze, the familiar strains of 'Dance Me to the End of Love'. I proceeded to drive across the dirt roads of that vineyard a little erratically, in desperate need of witnessing the song firsthand. I made it as the final verse began and proceeded to half-walk, half-run to the front of the stage. When I looked up I saw only the crew adjusting microphones and positioning fold back wedges. Okay, so the FOH mixer is tuning the PA, tweaking the EQs, I haven't actually missed anything. Relieved, I then wandered backstage and found Phil. We were both a little anxious; he'd bought Leonard an expensive and abundant bunch of native Australian flowers with the Susans' funds. Fine by me, lovely gesture, generous thought. It's no secret he has endless admiration and respect for LC and his writing, a collection of bootlegs, is well informed when it comes to Leonard's rewriting of lyrics to older songs: he's devoted.

Slowly the Cohen band emerged from their private tents and made their way to the stage. Leonard in dark sunglasses and a beret: cool, stylish, impeccably dressed, not bad for seventy-five. The sound was crisp, pristine, incredible. I watched from the side of stage and then from out front with a small gathering of ten or so people as the band worked through a dozen songs. Did I really need to see the actual concert now? This was just too good, so intimate, pure musical joy.

PK had also received permission from LC for The Susans to perform 'Memories', a song from *Death of a Ladies' Man*. Leonard was rumoured to have had less time for this album; he'd co-produced it with Phil Spector and they'd fought constantly during its inception. We had recorded 'Memories' for *All Souls Alive* back in 1993, with Dave McComb taking vocal duties. So we proceeded to play the song towards the end of our set with as much gusto as we could muster, a little overblown, perhaps. Still a rousing response from the amassed

Cohen followers, and we were pleased with ourselves that we performed a Leonard song for Leonard.

The Cohen concert was remarkable: the crowd hung on every word, laughed at every wisecrack and no doubt shed a tear or two. 'Who by Fire' spooked the bejesus out of me.

I'd brought along my vinyl copy of *Various Positions* and asked the promoter to have Leonard sign it for me, as was the protocol for the day. It was something I wasn't entirely comfortable with but, after missing out on my Johnny Cash moment, I wanted to at least have a memento of this occasion.

I was standing there in the backstage area, holding on to my LP. Some prick from the touring company was giving me grief for looking like some pathetic, desperate ageing fan. Sure, maybe I did look a little sad but Leonard signed my record and that's all that mattered.

He wrote, 'For Rob, fraternal greetings. Thanks for the flowers and the music. Leonard Cohen, Coldstream 2009.'

Phil Kakulas and Rob.

Moomoo

I met our neighbours from a few doors down the road through one of our wayward cats. One afternoon there was a knock on the door and there stood Renée and son Damon, both looking a little peeved. Moomoo had taken it upon herself to wander a few hundred metres down to their house, spray wee on the kids' bikes, fight the local stray cat, Patches (who was living under their house), and then finally bite and scratch one of their kids. Charming.

Moomoo was the most demanding, beautiful and vocal of cats: noisily announcing her arrival whenever she came in through the cat flap at whatever time she chose, meowing profusely for food or water, and again when she thought it was about time for us to fire up the heater or to hit the hay. She didn't like being cold and would often lie across the ducted heating vents happily baking her internal organs.

Peter had brought her out from the UK, this gorgeous chocolate-brown Burmese, a supermodel of sorts. He had paid an exorbitant amount of money and brought out her sister Shelby too: the feistier and lighter of the pair. On one occasion, my hand was dripping with blood after a playful pat with Shelby turned into my skin being shredded by her fast, powerful back claws.

Moomoo was far more affectionate than Shelby. She would graciously accept pats, rest close by you on the couch or on your lap when watching TV. Then, late at night, her favourite spot to lie down was smack-bang in the middle of my chest. Some mornings I woke up wondering if I was going to cough up a fur-ball. Her moist nose near my throat, she purred on repeat and gazed at me with her half-closed sleepy green eyes. Somehow, her centre of gravity made it feel like I was being slowly crushed by a massive boulder.

She lived a long time for a cat, our Moomoo: over twenty years. Sadly, she had kidney disease towards the end of her days. We changed her diet to a more effective type for cats experiencing renal failure, she had regular visits to the vet and then finally dialysis at home. Peter would hold her steady, relax her, and then slowly place the needle into the gathered flesh on the back of her neck. I'd hold and monitor the amount of saline solution trickling into her system. A cat on a drip. Who would have thought? Peter was determined, and would go to any lengths to care for and save Moomoo, the beloved beast.

Pigeons and Absinthe

After my father died, my brother and I somehow convinced our mother to visit Mark in Spain for the first time. Mark had been living in Madrid for over a decade and came back to Australia when he could. He'd landed on his feet, found his second home, immersed himself in the language and Spanish culture. He knew his way around his barrio and other interesting parts of Madrid and España.

The flight there was long. Mum hadn't been without a cigarette, apart from sleep, for quite some time, perhaps since she'd been pregnant with me, in fact. DVT was in the forefront of her mind too; every so often I'd wake up to find her balancing precariously over the armrests of sleeping passengers, trying to get to the aisle for a wander up and around the cabin. So nimble and fit was my mother, not bad at all for a 65 year-old.

Mark had arranged for us to take a driving holiday through Spain, with a few days in Portugal thrown in. September 11 happened the day prior to us heading off from Madrid. Mark rang from work, told us to switch on his TV and tune in to the breaking news. My mother and I watched the horror unfold on Spanish television, wondering what the hell was happening to the poor old world out there, such a harrowing sight.

Despite this we drove to incredible cities on our adventure: Lisbon, Seville, Granada, Valencia, Oporto, Bilboa and Barcelona. Barcelona was vibrant, brimming with visitors, loud, hectic, colourful.

Mark had arranged for us all to stay centrally, in a converted nunnery, all three of us in the one room. We were in a bar just off the infamous La Rambla, having a few drinks and a bite to eat; then our ma decided to retire to the safety of the convent walls for some respite from the noise and dizzying, transient nature of the place, but Mark had other ideas for me. We escorted Mum back to the hotel, then Mark took me to an absinthe bar to indulge in a mysterious green fairy or two.

Mark filled me in on a little history, the hallucinogenic properties, mentioned writers and artists who indulged, the banning of the drink. So we imbibed several, with me thinking after a time that I wasn't feeling any effects, or feeling remotely intoxicated. Having said all that, I couldn't remember getting into our hotel that night.

We hit the sack, knowing tomorrow would be a big day of sightseeing. We were surrounded by Gaudi creations, and our mother was most keen on visiting the fantastical Sagrada Família. Lights out.

I awoke the next day in a mild fog-laden haze, conscious of the room being very, very still and extremely quiet; there appeared to be an uncomfortable atmosphere, neither my brother nor mother was talking much. Slightly unusual. Apparently, in my sleep I had had rather vocal and loud, sexually charged dreams. There I was, sharing a room with my brother and mother, in a convent. This could not be good.

So the day began slowly and sheepishly, as we discovered Gaudi's unusual and free-flowing architecture: part Gothic, part modernist, part nature, part Disney nightmare. We were wandering the tops of buildings and up around curving stairwells and staircases, piecing together the sacred and the fanciful.

Our last stop was to be Park Güell, Gaudi Park. Mark and I were still feeling the effects of the night's boozing, but pushed on through the day so at least our mother could appreciate and see as much as possible. We arrived at Gaudi Park, with our goal being to walk up to the park's summit and to see the panoramic view of Barcelona from way up high. At the bottom of the path, a flock of pigeons were feeding on dark

berries from a tree. Mark, with utter madness, ran up and shook the branches frantically and we watched on as the poor unsuspecting birds flew off. Not quite sure what he was thinking, we proceeded along the path after calming him down. Higher and higher up to the promised, magnificent views, past the mosaic walls and Flintstone-like creations.

Finally, we reached the top and saw the ocean view ahead and the city behind us. Suddenly, it started to rain, but not raindrops. Above us circled the pigeons. They'd located their culprit and rained purple bird crap on him and his flock. Big purple blotches appeared on my mother's white cardigan and our jackets. Mark had worn his faithful leather coat, which he managed to clean effortlessly, but Ma and I continued the day dressed as we were, looking like two unfortunate derelicts with a penchant for purple.

My mother turned to us at one point and divulged that she thought it was our father. He didn't want us having too good a time without him.

España, 2001.
Rob and Mark.

Eyjafjallajökull

Peter received a phone call from his sister, Leisa, early morning London time. She was working at one of the major airlines and ringing from Melbourne with news that a cloud of volcanic ash from Iceland was spreading throughout European skies and beginning to cause havoc, prompting major delays at Heathrow Airport. If we didn't get going immediately we may just be stuck in London. So we got a move on, packed as quickly as possible and frantically headed out the door.

We'd been staying in a hotel in Earls Court, having a few days off before I was due to head off to Belgium for some shows with The Triffids and Peter was due to head back home. So, he scurried off to Heathrow and I scurried off to St Pancras. I booked a rail ticket to Hasselt via Brussels at an internet café and raced down to the Tube. Peter just made his flight home as I boarded my train.

The London show with The Triffids at the Barbican was superb, with UK additions Dev Hynes aka Lightspeed *Champion* and Stuart Staples from The Tindersticks added to the long list of Antipodeans celebrating the songwriting of

David McComb. It made for an incredible night: the band and the songs well received and Dave's memory and songwriting talent celebrated.

The Susans played a show at the Borderline the following night, along with The Nearly Brothers and Chris Abrahams and Melanie Oxley. It was a popular Mexican cantina–style basement venue in the heart of London. For us there was a sense the audience knew so many of the early songs intimately: a warmth, an anticipation. Magnificent.

For a time The Blackeyed Susans' album *Dedicated to the Ones We Love* enjoyed some airplay in cafés and bars around parts of Vienna. Our manager, DC, arranged a show at a popular venue called Fluc. It was a tight schedule and we planned to play there in between performing in Hasselt and leaving Belgium for the final show with The Triffids in Greece.

Peter in London, 2010.

The volcanic ash from Eyjafjallajökull was now causing airport closures and major disruptions to air travel throughout most of Europe. Essentially no-one was going anywhere by plane. I was trying to convince fellow band members we could drive 1000 kilometres plus overnight across Germany. Be there in Vienna in time to play, then drive back the following day and be back in time for our flight to Greece, if, in fact, the airports were again open and we'd be flying out.

I was receiving blank looks of complete disinterest; this was simply not going to happen. We were bunkered down in Hasselt unable to go anywhere. I had to let it go, move on and think about how the rest of this tour was going to pan out: when (and if) we'd eventually get home.

Christmas

I'd never met anyone who enjoyed Christmas this much, not ever. Peter embraced the giving and receiving of gifts like no other being. He enjoyed Christmas carols wholeheartedly, and insisted on having a real tree each year and a train circulating at its trunk, tooting out Christmas tunes.

I was even subjected to an all-night Christmas shopping extravaganza at Chadstone. I swear I had a panic attack within minutes of arriving. I just couldn't cope: not only with the hordes of people but the idea of having to make choices on 'things' and parting with wads of cash. It was all too overwhelming.

I'd spent the majority of my adult shopping hours in op shops so this shopping culture and cost was completely new to me. I quickly learnt I was just not a shopping guy. Fast-forward to recent times, when our friend Coty, Peter and I went shopping for a pencil case for two hours. Yes, really.

The Snarski family were a little more 'bah-humbug' and cynical about Christmas, but with the odd midnight mass thrown in. There'd be the occasional year when one of us would suggest a no-present year, so the day was anticlimactic: a little slow and a little sad.

Mum, however, would always put on an incredible spread on Christmas Eve, as was the Polish tradition. There was a mix of Polish fare and adaptations on more contemporary dishes, somehow managing to combine a taste of Asia with the sauerkraut and potato. My ma loves to cook and to provide – the food is never-ending – consequently you'd roll out of a chair after a delicious feast, slowly recover on a couch, unable to move or eat another thing. Then suddenly an array of rich desserts would be presented, my mother disappointed, curious as to why we couldn't indulge in her homemade pavlova or blackforest cake. My ma simply loves to feed people.

My only chore for the festive season at home with Peter is to order the tree, a big tree, the biggest tree they have. I don't even have to dress the tree, just order it and make sure it arrives with enough time to enjoy it. There are many, many baubles and decorations, some from Royal Doulton (I should know who, or what, that is). Each year it looks and smells incredible, with the scent of the fresh pine permeating through the house.

One year, after the tallest tree had arrived, it had been placed in its stand and adorned lovingly by Peter, every bit of tinsel in place. All I had to do was plonk the star on top. So I climbed up on a chair and stretched out as far as I could, and only then, by careful manipulation, just managed to place the star atop, with Peter, Coty and Siri looking on, advising from the sidelines below. Done: it was sitting there high above us all. Brilliant. We could now all go out for a coffee and a bite to eat and have a well-earned break from all this festiveness. There was a BES Christmas show that night too, which was pecking in the back of my brain, so we had just enough time to venture out and relax.

Two hours later, on our return, to our astonishment the tree had toppled forward and there were shattered baubles and pine needles strewn across the lounge-room floor with presents crushed beneath. Poor Peter. Poor me. Somehow it fell over a second time when I was trying to save my skin. It was suggested I obviously didn't do a good enough job of ruining Christmas the first time.

Peter's siblings had dubbed us Beryl and Lenny. Legend has it that Lenny was working up a sweat mowing the backyard one scorching afternoon when visitors turned up unannounced. Beryl yelled out from the kitchen window for Lenny to come in immediately and make the unexpected visitors a cup of tea. So, this was how we were seen, and yes: I was Lenny and Peter was Beryl.

When the Dalgleish family turned up for Christmas Day, I dared not go near the kitchen. I'm not sure how, but my cooking skills over the years had turned south. I feared the stovetop. I wasn't even sure I could blanch asparagus, so I stuck to the salads and fruit platter.

Drinking generally started when the family arrived, after exchanging greetings and salutations. I wasn't good at drinking in the daylight hours. To be honest, I wasn't good at drinking at any hour, even after all those years of practice. Still, I went with the flow.

After the meal, the kids and adults received their presents and generally there was a lot of banter and carry-on, all very social and good natured. One year I was made to dress up as Santa without warning. I had no choice, Craig was always recognised by the kids, so all insisted it had to be me. I handed out the presents and ho-ho-hoed: something I'd never imagined myself doing.

One particular Christmas at our place, Bev, matriarch of the family, had fallen ill and retired to our room. All the kids thought it was attention-seeking behaviour on their mother's part so she was stubbornly ignored by her kids as she lay

moaning in our bed. Occasionally I checked on her but she just wanted to sleep and drink water. As the day progressed, we had had our fair share of booze: a story here, a song there, a joke or two. The neighbours came, the neighbours went, and we all got increasingly louder. In the meantime, I'd somehow managed to fall over and roll down a hill out the back; bits of grass were still clinging to my clothes.

Someone then started up a word game that I couldn't quite get the grip of: 'I went to the shop and I bought a _____'.

The family would clap and cheer when you had the correct answer, louder and with more and more enthusiasm as the game progressed, or boo and jeer harshly when you were wrong. After many, many rounds, I still didn't get it. I was getting slightly agitated and slunk off to the bathroom, as this was getting painful. Peter followed me down the hallway to share the puzzle, as it was becoming a little too excruciating even for him. It was just so simple: use the first letter of your Christian name, is all. Peter Senior had 'gone to the shop to buy a prostitute', and I still hadn't cottoned on, for God's sake.

When it next came around to my turn, I feigned the wrong answer until it came around again full circle. I didn't want to give it away so obviously that I'd been told. Then the second time through I snapped and let fly.

'I went to the shop and I bought a robot and a raccoon, and you're all a bunch of fucking cunts!'

Nice. This was Peter's family I was barking at, including the lovely aunt and uncle from the Gold Coast. They took it with a grain of salt, thought it was quite hilarious that I'd got so riled and rollickingly drunk. Luckily for me, their Scottish bawdiness was prone to a bit of misbehaving, though I sensed the lovely Aunt Agnes wasn't so sure.

Lesson learnt, I never again drank at a Christmas gathering or placed the star on the tree.

Hometown Farewells

I don't think anything hits you as hard or reminds you of your age and own mortality as returning to the place you grew up. As the years go by elsewhere, on returning you feel more disconnected, distant; there's almost a sense of being repelled by your own hometown. Buildings appear, people disappear, friends' kids seem to finish school, university, leave home, travel overseas, when in the back of your mind, you're thinking they must be fast approaching high school. Time moves in an odd, mysterious way.

Peter convinced me that my mother would love to return to Perth for a visit after years of her resistance. I simply believed what I'd heard over time, which was always a swift, dismissive and decisive 'No, I couldn't', followed by a series of all-too-difficult scenarios created in my mother's mind. Peter saw through all this, convinced her it would be easy; he'd take her himself on the plane and she could stay with us in the hotel in downtown Perth and we'd venture out and about, though absolutely nothing she didn't want to do.

Mum loved returning and seeing some old familiar faces and places. Mark and I were singing as guests with The Triffids at the Perth International Arts Festival, on the foreshore overlooking the Swan River. She enjoyed some theatre with Peter, we visited old friends, dined out, and on the last day we took a cruise along the Swan. That river carried some wonderful memories of when our family first arrived in Perth in 1966. She used to take Mark and I as toddlers to a little strip of river beach in South Perth where we'd play and paddle, make sandcastles and soak up the sun. Mum could see it from the ferry and these memories took hold and took her breath away. She swooned, flooded by the images of the past, drained by the years gone by.

I had a very similar experience when I was the ripe old age of thirty-six, having landed back in Perth for a tour. That age was significant to me. I'd somehow remembered that the median age for a male's life expectancy, from my high school days, was seventy-two, so it was a fair indication in my mind – though times have changed – that I was pretty much halfway through.

I decided to take myself off on a drive to revisit some life-defining childhood haunts. I drove through Armadale, down Seventh Road, past our lonesome old house, then past Neerigen Brook Primary, which of course looked remarkably smaller (I was Head Boy there: obviously the election process was flawed), then past Kelmscott High, and up along the Brookton Highway, which led to our old farm and orchard in Karragullen.

The trees rushed by, orchards appeared, houses disappeared and the gaps between properties grew. There was less of the orchard: more land, less fencing and fewer paddocks, and a new house added on towards the back of the farm. Our family house looked the same, but different. The surroundings had changed enough for it to morph into a cold, distant, unfamiliar dwelling. I leant over the gate, looked at the dam I used to swim across, then up and out across the steep hill where we'd run as our father coached from the balcony. I looked straight down the gravel road leading to our old home. After a while my reminiscing began to push me away, send me back to wherever it was I came.

Just before I headed off, I caught a glimpse of our old wooden letterbox, which my father had made. There, in my own handwriting, that of the ten-year-old boy, the numbers 151. I felt sapped, wounded, and time began to swirl. All it took was seeing those three naïve handwritten numerals for me to feel my age. I slowly regained my faculties, got back into the car and drove away, wondering if I was about halfway through.

The house, Karragullen.

Live

My brother played a cracking solo set supporting Mick Thomas and his band The Roving Commission. Skyscraper Stan and the Commission Flats were on the bill too, old sounds for a young band. Their singer, a giant of a man, moved like Mr Squiggle and sang like a bird. I kept wondering which era these guys had sprung from…and how. Mick was in fine form too. The crowd danced, Mick joked; he drew the audience in with charming wit and banter.

I wandered towards the exit after the encores. The crowd dispersed and I saw Mick there at the merchandise desk, signing CDs. He smiled, thanked me for coming along and said in a humble, optimistic tone, 'Isn't it great that people still come to see us?'

That simple comment rang like a giant bell in the empty space between my ears. It's true: it's heart-warming, astonishing, and some nights are overwhelming. I'd never experienced foot-stomping for an encore until JP Shilo and I performed the songs from *Wounded Bird* above the Astor Theatre in Perth. The warmth received from the audience that night reached another climate – somehow helped along by Jenny Czech, the most enthusiastic sleigh-bell ringer on the tour thus far, and also by knowing so many people in the room, if not by name, by sight.

The launch for the album in Melbourne at the Spotted Mallard was the calmest I'd ever felt at a show. To walk through an audience and recognise so many people from past and present, you can't help but feel buoyed by the amount of support people show you; it's palpable, you can sense it from the stage.

The turnout for The Blackeyed Susans (with a string ensemble) at the 2016 Sydney Festival was beyond expectations: an audience so appreciative, the stars aligned. Incredible. Lucky to still be able to play music and, yes, isn't it great that people still come to hear the songs and we have partners and family who support us to do what we love.

J.P. Shilo and Rob.

Alcohol

Thankfully, I don't drink anymore. I actually remember things – lyrics, chords, events, my past, what happened the night before and what I've said and done – well, mostly. I've not had to lie down on a cold piece of concrete to stop the world from spinning for a very long time, or fallen face-first over tram tracks or passed out under a tree amongst the masses at a music festival. I've not tried to pick anyone up (apologies to those) or thrown anything at anyone either (apologies again) for quite some time. I don't talk half as much drivel and hopefully I don't bore people with endless, incredulous babbling.

I highly recommend sobriety and, quite frankly, I was never all that good at boozing anyway. I could be an absolute prick. I have my suspicions that a couple of managers slipped away quietly because of my rubbish behaviour.

Over the years I had a few dry spells but I weaned myself off eventually. This time I was drinking spritzers, and the balance of sparkling water was gradually overtaking the ‹savblonk›. I honestly felt like I'd started slurring my words even before I tilted meagre amounts of wine into my humble glass of bubbles. There seemed to be a powerful psychological effect playing with my simple, sober mind. I no longer have hangovers, I like to be out and about during daylight hours, I'm not quite as awful and, in short, I seem to be more productive.

So much of my social life revolved around alcohol, it was difficult to escape. Bars, parties, dinners, barbeques. I suggested once that we go out to a café in the morning for my birthday. Close friends and family thought I'd completely lost the plot. A quick coffee, a chat and a see-you-next-year would've been just fine, but it didn't quite eventuate.

Ah well, *Na zdrowie!*

Punters Club, Fitzroy 2002.
Glenn Richards, Dan Luscombe and Rob.

Golden Boy

Harvey was lying in his comfy dog bed; still warm, no longer breathing. His sister, Peggy, lay by his side snoring, totally unaware. My tears began to flow, and I started to choke up, I could barely get the words out to Peter, still half-asleep in bed. Our Golden Boy had died.

Peter's best pal Coty was staying overnight; she came out of the spare room with tousled hair, still in her pyjamas to see what all the commotion was about.

Harvey had not been well for some time. Several months before, he'd started to experience seizures; he had a range of medications but there were seemingly more complications. Occasionally there were pools of blood on the floor and Harvey had recently started to spend time hiding in the back of his kennel. There was a foreboding sense of the inevitable. Still, it didn't make it any easier to say goodbye or to prepare for his departure.

For several days afterwards I had vivid flashbacks, and I'd find photos as I scrolled through my phone. I'd send one off to Peter, and he'd send another one to me. It was difficult;

it would take some time to let go. One photograph always killed me. Peter is in the background on his laptop, with Betty (another pooch) at his side, both by a pile of garden debris ready for a burn-off. I'm in the foreground and Harvey is licking my forehead as I lie there on the grassy slope in the backyard. It just reminded me of our boy's gentle and giving nature. He was the only male in our pack of pooches and cats, the boy often left behind as the demands of the girls far outweighed his needs. On occasions he'd come up to you with that lovely smiling face, tongue hanging out, wagging his bushy, golden tail, reminding us he was also there. A pat, just a little bit of attention wouldn't be a bad thing. His response was pure joy, and he would growl a light, gentle warning to any of the other demanding beasts that encroached on his moment.

We had so many pets when we were growing up, but I don't think I ever truly appreciated the character and individual nature of dogs until more recent years. Harvey's death hurt a lot. I felt I could relate to that old adage of learning from animals and came to appreciate more the sorrow others felt when their pets perished and the hollowness that was left.

Harvey

Pledge

I'd started fulfilling my pledges. Taking people out for a coffee, throwing together the occasional promised vegetarian frittata and performing acoustically in the lounge rooms of kind folk around Melbourne, Adelaide, Sydney and Perth. All of this for the sake of financing and completing the much-maligned recording of *Wounded Bird*.

My manager-guy, Andrew Fuller, had explained the process, set it up and started the ball rolling, feeling quietly confident.

It was surprisingly enjoyable, this crowd-funding business, something I didn't expect to embrace. Initially I was bullish and reluctant; I resisted the idea, wasn't sure if I was the right type of personality to throw myself into it. Who goes into someone's house, stands in the middle of their lounge room, talks about their songs and warbles away? Well, I guess I do.

I found myself enjoying these lounge-room gatherings more than standing two foot higher on a stage in a pub somewhere. Ultimately the host wants you to be comfortable in their home, they want to enjoy their time and have their friends there to share the music. It couldn't be more intimate and I couldn't have felt more exposed if I tried – voice, guitar, an anecdote or two, zero amplification.

The response to the Pledge Campaign took me by surprise. Somehow the funds to complete the recording were raised within a week of its inception, so humbling I nearly burst into tears. Now I simply had to fulfil the remaining promised obligations.

Luckily, the first of the acoustic house concerts was at a friend's place. Sandy was a charming and gregarious host and laid on an incredible spread. He placed chairs in an arc facing the corner where I'd stand and warble. It was easier than I expected to sing for the friends he'd gathered together on that Sunday afternoon in Seddon; I knew half of them.

One other promised pledge was to record people's favourite songs in a modest fashion onto my iPhone and email the recordings back. The songs weren't meticulously recorded; I'd simply find a room in the house where I could strum and sing without too much aural interference from the television or various creatures inside or out. Having said that, there are ambient sounds from the house popping up all over the place. A snoring dog, birds singing outside, cat bells, television mumblings are all captured in the background of *Low Fidelity*. Producer / guitarist Shane O'Mara thought it was part charming, majorly irritating. I never intended to release these recordings once I began, anyway, but I was growing quite fond of the eclectic mix of song requests from folk around the globe. The big classics, the obscure minor hits, the old, the contemporary.

I found myself occasionally replaying this growing collection of tunes late at night, with the iPhone plonked on my bedside table. There was something honest and pure, intimate and flawed about them, they captured something else. I wanted to know if anyone else heard that, or felt the same way.

JP Shilo likened them to a black-and-white snapshot from a photo booth, not to be tampered with, caught in a moment. Shane, on the other hand, relished the challenge of a tinker, an opportunity to embellish the songs. It was like discovering a new and unusual recording frontier. Man walks on moon; man makes record on iPhone.

Shane had a multitude of ideas, and the sound palette at this point was almost a blank canvas: I'd formed the outlines, a rudimentary sketch, and he could splash whatever colours he chose. We were at Yikesville Studio listening to his initial overdubs. I'd given him free rein, he worked without hindrance

and with little direction. I enjoyed working this way – less arm wrestling, less of my interference, less responsibility. I'd already relinquished part of my responsibility when I'd given the pledge folk the ability to choose any song they thought worthy. My only strong opinion when mixing was to pan some of my original recordings to the extreme left and Shane's additions to the extreme right in some circumstances, just to give the sound more scope in its limited capacity.

We'd already voted some songs out. I don't think anyone else needed to hear my acapella version of 'Danny Boy' and as much as I liked The Babies as a young teenager, John Wait's 'Missing You' was completely missing me. I couldn't find a way in; it didn't suit my voice or range and I felt I'd failed to deliver on that one altogether, another song for the cutting-room floor.

Shane O'Mara and Rob, Yikesville 2015.

Writing songs

I don't feel qualified enough to set down my theories on songwriting. I haven't written that many, really, and, in all honesty, it still remains a mystery to me. I've only ever set out to write a song with a particular subject matter in mind on a handful of occasions. I've collaborated with musicians who work well in this way. But when I write alone in this manner, it can often be a fruitless and taxing exercise. It's draining, it gives me a headache and I don't have the patience or the ability. I often feel that when a stubborn song does emerge through this process, it can often sound forced and a little clumsy. I'm by no means prolific, possibly because of this laidback work ethic of mine; I tend to wait for a song.

I write fragments or short anecdotes with a purpose or plot in mind, but, for whatever reason, not songs – not quite, anyway. There's something in the initial part, the inspiration, that's inexplicable and quite random. It's as if the song starts to write itself, and I'm merely a vessel to bring it to the shore. Melodies curl and float through the air and land in my lap. Lyrics come from pretty much anywhere: something seen, something read, something thought, or words simply fall out of my mouth or appear on a scrap of paper or a page in a diary. I just happen to be there with a pen in hand.

I've heard Brian Wilson, Shane MacGowan and Townes Van Zant talk about songwriting in a similar esoteric manner. Music and lyrics seem to come from somewhere else.

Having said all that, I like a song to make sense. I'm partial to a beginning, middle and end. I'm old school. If the lyrics work well on a page, generally for me they work well within the soundscape of a song.

Caravan Music Club

I've played the Caravan Music Club in sunny Oakleigh quite a few times now. Lovely: old-style stage up high with an ornate arch, immaculate acoustics and crisp, clear sound system. It's on a quiet street in the eastern suburbs of Melbourne, nestled between a Greek restaurant precinct and a busy highway that's sometimes used as a drag strip for those wayward youths struggling to find better things to do late at night.

I got the impression that Peter Foley, the owner, cared about how music was presented here. He wandered about during sound check, lighting tea candles on the tables he'd covered in red chequered tablecloths. It has that old-school comfort.

However, it was also attached to a Returned Servicemen's League and I always found myself having to take my hat on and off repeatedly until I worked out how not to cross the line of the RSL floor plan. No disrespect intended but I wear hats often, incessantly. If I could sleep in a hat I would, and on occasions I do. Why is there not a solution? We can beam images of Saturn's surface back to Earth but we can't find a cure for hair loss. Vanity ... it's stupid... I'm stupid.

On one occasion, I was slotted in as the musical support for the quick-witted Jewish cowboy, writer and musician Kinky Friedman. He was dressed head to toe in black – cowboy hat, cowboy boots – and drawing on a monstrous cigar outside the venue's doors as I rolled up for sound check. Music aside, for me the highlight of his set came from a short story he read about his father. Moving, poignant, honest.

This time around I was the opening act for Toni Childs, '80s icon and one of my dad's favourite singers. He found the quality of her voice interesting and unique. I remember him saying something along the lines of 'She's the female Gene Pitney'. Toni, on this night and the previous, decided to treat her crowd to a preview of her new songs from a forthcoming release and leave the hits behind: brave, considering some of her audience hadn't been out since 1988 and were here essentially to hear the songs they knew and loved.

I finished my set. The audience were polite, attentive and appreciative. Those gathered applauded enough to make me feel okay about being the singer guy in the support slot, so I packed my gear and relaxed in the band room. Hat on head, I emerged later in the night, listened and watched Toni Childs, thinking her new songs were being well received.

Later again, I found myself out the front of the venue in an exhausting, one-sided conversation with a rather inebriated lass who was in desperate need of a cigarette. By this point, some not-so-happy fans had started to slowly wander out and leave, a little agitated by Toni's choice to perform new material. They were wanting to hear her popular songs and their patience was wearing thin. It was getting slightly awkward, as the drunken stranger was now earnestly and a little aggressively trying to convince the folk leaving that Ms Childs would in fact be playing all the hits and they shouldn't abandon her as she was a wonderful artist, expressing some of her innermost thoughts and feelings. But nothing she could've said would convince this handful of disgruntled patrons, who continued walking off into the night.

'She's great. You can't go yet, you don't understand. She's an artist. No, really, I mean, that support guy, he was shithouse but she's wonderful...'

At this juncture she slowly turned to me, her scrambled thoughts and arrant confusion reached out to a moment of clarity. Now, half-remembering, she slurred sheepishly, 'What was your name again?'

Acknowledgements

I'm not sure whether I should thank or blame Jon Tarry and Terri-ann White, the two people who prompted me into print. I'll thank them for now, especially Terri-ann for her boundless tolerance and patience when it came to dealing with my inexperience in this field and handling the occasional hiccup with aplomb.

Special thanks to Peter Dalgleish, Maria Snarski, the brother, Andrew Fuller, Pony Webster, DC, Shane O'Mara, the Dalgleish clan, Freya Elizabeth, Tory Drexel-Bates, Nigel Harford, Siri Umpherston, Sioux and Tim, all the photographers and artists who contributed images especially Denise Nestor and her family, The Blackeyed Susans, Judith Lucy, Andrew Squire, The Triffids, Chad's Tree, J.P. Shilo … and anyone else I've overlooked who prodded me along.

Cover photograph moustache concept originally created by Siriporn Umpherston.

Photographic acknowledgements

We thank the following for the use of their images.
Copyright remains with the photographer.

Snarski family archive	Pages 8, 14, 17, 20, 26, 36, 102, 110, 122, 123, 134
Rob Snarski	Pages 23, 28, 40, 47, 58, 125, 143 (selfie)
Denise Nestor	Pages 12, 75, 107
Kym Cohen	Pages 43, 70
Coo Bennett	Page 56
Bleddyn Butcher	Page 65
Sharon West	Page 68
Scott Wajon	Page 78
Robert Frith	Page 84
Joanne Alach	Page 87
Steve Appel	Page 117
Robert Hall	Page 119
Peter Dalgleish	Pages 130, 140
L. J. Spruyt	Page 133
Tim McNeilage	Page 138
Andrew Watson (Semiconductor Media)	Pages 144, 146

www.ingramcontent.com/pod-product-compliance
Lightning Source LLC
Chambersburg PA
CBHW030220170426
43194CB00007BA/802